The Terrorist Attack on America

Other books in the Current Controversies series:

The Terrorist Attack on America

Mary E. Williams, *Book Editor*

Daniel Leone, *President*
Bonnie Szumski, *Publisher*
Scott Barbour, *Managing Editor*

CURRENT CONTROVERSIES

GREENHAVEN
PRESS®

THOMSON
™
GALE

San Diego • Detroit • New York • San Francisco • Cleveland
New Haven, Conn. • Waterville, Maine • London • Munich

LIBRARY OF CONGRESS CATALOGING-IN-PUBLICATION DATA

The terrorist attack on America / Mary E. Williams, book editor.
    p. cm. — (Current controversies)
    Includes bibliographical references and index.
    ISBN 0-7377-1324-0 (lib. bdg. : alk. paper) —
    ISBN 0-7377-1325-9 (pbk. : alk. paper)
    1. September 11 Terrorist Attacks, 2001. 2. Terrorism—United States—Prevention. 3. Civil rights—United States. 4. United States—Politics and government—2001– . I. Williams, Mary E., 1960– . II. Series.
    HV6432 .T4735 2003
    973.931—dc21
                                                                2002070613

Printed in the United States of America

Contents

went unheeded because Americans—exhausted from their vigilance during the Cold War—had grown cynical about the national interest and instead busied themselves with materialism, consumption, and entertainment.

Chapter 2: Is Anger Toward America Justified?

Yes: Anger Toward America Is Justified

people. Moreover, the United States and its wealthy allies are responsible for most of the war, genocide, and human rights violations in recent history. The people of the world must reject all forms of extremism and fundamentalism.

No: Anger Toward America Is Not Justified

Chapter 3: Are Measures Against Terrorism a Threat to Civil Liberties?

Yes: Measures Against Terrorism Threaten Civil Liberties

bunals gives the U.S. attorney general the power to investigate people for any reason and to use secret evidence that is not admissible in regular civilian courts.

No: Measures Against Terrorism Do Not Threaten Civil Liberties

Chapter 4: How Should America Respond to Terrorism?

should be found and prosecuted, but war should be avoided because it kills innocent people and feeds the cycle of violence.

Foreword

By definition, controversies are "discussions of questions in which opposing opinions clash" (Webster's Twentieth Century Dictionary Unabridged). Few would deny that controversies are a pervasive part of the human condition and exist on virtually every level of human enterprise. Controversies transpire between individuals and among groups, within nations and between nations. Controversies supply the grist necessary for progress by providing challenges and challengers to the status quo. They also create atmospheres where strife and warfare can flourish. A world without controversies would be a peaceful world; but it also would be, by and large, static and prosaic.

The Series' Purpose

The purpose of the Current Controversies series is to explore many of the social, political, and economic controversies dominating the national and international scenes today. Titles selected for inclusion in the series are highly focused and specific. For example, from the larger category of criminal justice, Current Controversies deals with specific topics such as police brutality, gun control, white collar crime, and others. The debates in Current Controversies also are presented in a useful, timeless fashion. Articles and book excerpts included in each title are selected if they contribute valuable, long-range ideas to the overall debate. And wherever possible, current information is enhanced with historical documents and other relevant materials. Thus, while individual titles are current in focus, every effort is made to ensure that they will not become quickly outdated. Books in the Current Controversies series will remain important resources for librarians, teachers, and students for many years.

In addition to keeping the titles focused and specific, great care is taken in the editorial format of each book in the series. Book introductions and chapter prefaces are offered to provide background material for readers. Chapters are organized around several key questions that are answered with diverse opinions representing all points on the political spectrum. Materials in each chapter include opinions in which authors clearly disagree as well as alternative opinions in which authors may agree on a broader issue but disagree on the possible solutions. In this way, the content of each volume in Current Controversies mirrors the mosaic of opinions encountered in society. Readers will quickly realize that there are many viable answers to these complex issues. By questioning each author's conclusions, students and casual readers can begin to develop the critical thinking skills so important to evaluating opinionated material.

Current Controversies is also ideal for controlled research. Each anthology in the series is composed of primary sources taken from a wide gamut of informational categories including periodicals, newspapers, books, United States and foreign government documents, and the publications of private and public organizations. Readers will find factual support for reports, debates, and research papers covering all areas of important issues. In addition, an annotated table of contents, an index, a book and periodical bibliography, and a list of organizations to contact are included in each book to expedite further research.

Perhaps more than ever before in history, people are confronted with diverse and contradictory information. During the Persian Gulf War, for example, the public was not only treated to minute-to-minute coverage of the war, it was also inundated with critiques of the coverage and countless analyses of the factors motivating U.S. involvement. Being able to sort through the plethora of opinions accompanying today's major issues, and to draw one's own conclusions, can be a complicated and frustrating struggle. It is the editors' hope that Current Controversies will help readers with this struggle.

Greenhaven Press anthologies primarily consist of previously published material taken from a variety of sources, including periodicals, books, scholarly journals, newspapers, government documents, and position papers from private and public organizations. These original sources are often edited for length and to ensure their accessibility for a young adult audience. The anthology editors also change the original titles of these works in order to clearly present the main thesis of each viewpoint and to explicitly indicate the opinion presented in the viewpoint. These alterations are made in consideration of both the reading and comprehension levels of a young adult audience. Every effort is made to ensure that Greenhaven Press accurately reflects the original intent of the authors included in this anthology.

Introduction

On the morning of September 11, 2001, hijackers took control of four commercial airliners outbound from cities in the northeastern United States. They intentionally crashed two planes into the World Trade Center towers in New York City and one plane into the Pentagon building near Washington, D.C. The fourth plane, which was likely heading for the White House, crashed into a field in western Pennsylvania. Thousands were killed in the most devastating act of terrorism that had ever occurred on American soil.

Images of the attack were harrowing. Each of the collisions into the World Trade Center—and the ensuing fires and rescue efforts—were captured on film and broadcast around the world. Americans watched in shock and horror as the two 110-story buildings collapsed and as smoke from the wreckage enshrouded the lower Manhattan skyline. Three days later, Congress passed a resolution authorizing the use of military force to find and retaliate against those responsible for the attack. President George W. Bush asserted that the terrorists had committed "an act of war" against "freedom itself."

September 11 was not the first time that the twin towers had been targeted by terrorists. On February 26, 1993, a bomb was detonated in a basement garage of the World Trade Center, killing six and injuring thousands. The perpetrators, who were eventually caught and sentenced to prison, were followers of Sheikh Omar Abdel Rahman and had intended to attack the United Nations headquarters and several other New York City landmarks. Rahman was the spiritual leader of the Islamic Group, a militant organization that would later claim responsibility for a 1995 attempt to assassinate Egyptian president Hosni Mubarak and a 1997 attack in Luxor, Egypt, that killed fifty-eight foreign tourists. The 1993 bombing of the World Trade Center was provoked by Rahman's indignation over what he felt were corrupting Western influences in Egypt and other largely Muslim countries. In addition, Rahman and his followers were angry about the U.S. alliance with Israel. (Territorial disputes between Israel and its neighboring Arab countries, as well as the unresolved status of the Palestinian Arabs living in Israeli-occupied regions, have been a source of conflict in the Middle East since the late 1940s.) Some Muslim fundamentalists consider Jews, Christians, and other non-Muslims to be "infidels" with cultures that undermine traditional Islamic tenets. Radical fundamentalists, whom most analysts claim are not representative of mainstream Islam, have often main-

13

tained that they must rid the Muslim world of infidels and state leaders who co-operate with Western governments.

As with the 1993 bombing, the September 11 attack was traced to Muslim extremists. In a nationally televised address before Congress on September 20, 2001, President George W. Bush announced that "the evidence we have gathered all points to a collection of loosely affiliated terrorist organizations known as al-Qaeda." Al-Qaeda—an Arabic term for "the base"—is a globally operating network that officials believe is headed by Saudi Arabian exile Osama bin Laden.

Born into a wealthy Saudi family, bin Laden was heir to a fortune—currently estimated to be worth over $200 million—after the death of his construction tycoon father. In 1979, bin Laden moved to Afghanistan to join that country's U.S.-supported guerilla war against a Soviet invasion. His formerly moderate political views shifted during his participation in the ten-year conflict, growing increasingly radical as he fought alongside Islamic fundamentalists with anti-Western sentiments. In the mid-1980s, bin Laden joined forces with Palestinian Muslim Brotherhood leader Abdallah Azzam to form the Services Office, an organization that funneled weapons and fighters to the Afghan resistance. The Services Office established recruitment centers around the world that enlisted and transported thousands of men from over fifty countries to Afghanistan to fight the Soviets; it also constructed and funded paramilitary training camps in Afghanistan and Pakistan. The resources that the Services Office brought to the conflict helped Afghanistan expel the Soviets in the late 1980s.

Wanting to support Muslim resistance movements in Saudi Arabia and Yemen and extend his recruitment and training operations into more countries, bin Laden allegedly formed al-Qaeda in 1988. When Services Office cofounder Azzam was killed by a car bomb in 1989, the Services Office split into two factions, and the extremist faction joined al-Qaeda. After the end of the Afghan-Soviet war, bin Laden also forged alliances with several other militant Muslim groups—including the Islamic Group, the organization that was to be implicated in the 1993 World Trade Center bombing.

In the early 1990s, bin Laden strongly denounced Saudi Arabia for allowing American troops into its borders during the Persian Gulf War. That conflict, a U.S.-led battle in response to Iraq's invasion of Kuwait, was supported by Saudi Arabia and other Middle Eastern governments that were concerned about Iraq's destabilizing influence in the region. Bin Laden and other militant fundamentalists, however, considered the presence of "infidel" American troops in Saudi Arabia a form of blasphemy because Saudi Arabia was the birthplace of Islam's founder, the prophet Muhammad, and the home of Islam's most sacred site, the city of Mecca. Bin Laden's criticism, as well as pressure from the governments of Algeria and Yemen, led the Saudi government to strip him of his citizenship in 1994.

While living in exile in Sudan, Africa, bin Laden most likely began drawing up plans for terrorist strikes against U.S. interests. Bin Laden is presumed to have been behind the 1995 bombing of a joint U.S.-Saudi army training facility in Riyadh, Saudi Arabia, which killed five Americans and two Indians. A 1996 bombing of a military apartment building in Dahran, Saudi Arabia, which killed nineteen U.S. airmen and injured several hundred Americans and Saudi Arabians, was also attributed to bin Laden and his associates. Under pressure from the United States, Saudi Arabia, and the United Nations, Sudan expelled bin Laden in 1996. He found refuge in Afghanistan, which was then under the rule of the Taliban, a Muslim fundamentalist regime.

The Taliban, a militant sect of religious students that had previously fought in the Afghan-Soviet conflict, gained U.S. support when it rose to power in 1996 because it was initially perceived as pro-Western. The United States grew wary, however, after human rights and women's groups began criticizing the Taliban's governmental policies. Of particular concern was the Taliban's suppression of women, who were ordered to leave their jobs, abandon educational pursuits, and wear burqas—clothing covering the entire body—when venturing outside. The U.S. view turned distinctly negative after Osama bin Laden forged an alliance with the Taliban and persuaded its leaders to adopt an overtly anti-Western stance. According to Pakistani journalist Ahmed Rashid, Afghanistan became "a haven for international terrorism" by the late 1990s, "and the Americans and the West were at a loss for how to handle it."

In August 1998, the U.S. embassies in Nairobi, Kenya, and Dar es Salaam, Tanzania, were simultaneously bombed, killing 263 people, including twelve Americans, and injuring more than five thousand others. U.S. investigators soon traced the attack to bin Laden's network, and, in retaliation, President Bill Clinton ordered military air strikes on suspected terrorist-related facilities in Afghanistan and Sudan. Though policy makers generally supported the air strikes at the time, many have criticized the attacks in retrospect because they apparently failed to impede bin Laden's terrorist network. Some even feel that the U.S. counterstrike intensified anti-Western attitudes among radical Muslims, enhancing bin Laden's appeal. As Sudanese scholar Abdulrahman Abuzayd stated after the U.S. retaliation, "The Americans have suddenly created a Muslim hero out of [bin Laden], whereas last week he was considered a fanatic nut."

In October 2000, two years after the embassy bombings, a small boat exploded next to the navy destroyer USS *Cole* while it was refueling in Aden, Yemen. The blast, which killed seventeen sailors and wounded thirty-nine others, was eventually attributed to suicide bombers connected with bin Laden's network. In the ensuing months—up through the summer of 2001—the U.S. government issued an alert warning Americans of an increased possibility of terrorism against travelers and U.S. interests abroad. The alert was nonspecific, however, and provided no forewarning of the events of September 11, 2001.

In the wake of the September 11 attack, President Bush officially declared a "war on terror," directed not only against terrorist groups but also against nations that provide refuge to terrorists. Bush announced that "any nation that continues to harbor or support terrorism will be regarded by the United States as a hostile regime." Consequently, as soon as officials determine that al-Qaeda was most likely the group responsible for the attack, they demanded that the Taliban hand over bin Laden and his associates. The Taliban refused, and in October 2001, the United States began bombing various Taliban and al-Qaeda targets in Afghanistan and providing weapons and assistance to the Northern Alliance, a coalition of Afghan opposition forces. By the end of 2001, the Taliban regime had been toppled, numerous al-Qaeda members had been killed or captured, and an interim Afghan government had been established. The whereabouts of Osama bin Laden, however, remained unknown.

As this volume goes to press, bin Laden has not publicly admitted that he or his al-Qaeda network were responsible for the September 11 attack. However, in several videotaped interviews that have surfaced since the attack, bin Laden has made statements implying that he knew of and enthusiastically supported plans to crash hijacked planes into buildings. He has also expressed why he believes such terrorism is justified, and his reasoning echoes the thinking of Omar Rahman, the cleric who had instigated the 1993 bombing of the World Trade Center. In a taped statement that aired on an Arab television station on October 7, 2001, bin Laden maintained that Americans "have abused the blood, honor and sanctuaries of Muslims," arguing that the terrorist attack was God's punishment for the U.S.-backed sanctions against Iraq and for the U.S. support of the Israeli occupation of Palestinian land. He proclaimed that "neither America nor the people who live in it will dream of security before we live it in Palestine, and not before all the infidel armies leave the land of Muhammad."

Bin Laden's antagonism toward America may indicate a level of frustration and anti-Western resentment in the Muslim world that is more widespread than previously thought. In the years to come, the United States will face difficult challenges as it struggles to fight radical Islamic terrorism without alienating the growing populations of Muslims living in various parts of the world. This volume, which presents opinions from commentators representing different points on the political spectrum, provides an introductory overview of the causes, consequences, and responses to the terrorist attack on America.

Chapter 1

What Caused the Terrorist Attack on America?

Chapter Preface

Since the autumn of 2001, various politicians, scholars, and media figures have speculated about the root causes of the September 11 terrorist attack on America. Most accept the U.S. government's determinations that al-Qaeda, the international terrorist network headed by the radical Muslim fundamentalist Osama bin Laden, was responsible for the attack. Yet experts continue to debate what role religion and culture played in motivating extremists to participate in such devastating suicide raids.

Some analysts maintain that the September 11 attack was one result of a basic and long-standing incompatibility between Islamic culture and Western civilization. In an often-cited and controversial 1993 article, Harvard professor Samuel P. Huntington defined the increase in radical Islamic terrorism during the twentieth century as evidence of a deep rift among the world's major civilizations—a division he believed would influence international relations in the near future:

> The principal conflicts of global politics will occur between nations and groups of different civilizations. The clash of civilizations will be the battle lines of the future. . . .
>
> [The] centuries-old military interaction between the West and Islam is unlikely to decline. It could become more virulent. The Gulf War left some Arabs feeling proud that [Iraqi leader] Saddam Hussein had attacked Israel and stood up to the West. It also left many feeling humiliated and resentful of the West's military presence in the Persian Gulf, the West's overwhelming military dominance, and their apparent inability to shape their own destiny.

Adding credence to the "clash of civilizations" theory is the fact that Islamist [militant fundamentalist] movements have increasingly relied on religious justifications for launching attacks on the largely secular West. In the 1980s the Ayatollah Khomeini, the first clerical leader of Iran's fundamentalist government, called for a jihad, or holy war, against the "great Satan," America. In a similar vein, in October 2001, Osama bin Laden claimed that "unjust" U.S. policies in the Middle East had "divided the whole world into two sides—the side of believers and the side of infidels. . . . Every Muslim has to rush to make his religion victorious." Some analysts contend that Western values, which promote representative government, individual liberties, and church-state separation, are undeniably at odds with an Islamic tendency to reject democracy and religious pluralism.

Many experts, however, reject the "clash of civilizations" theory for being overly simplistic. Moderate Muslim clerics and scholars insist that the beliefs and actions of militant fundamentalists represent only the radical fringes of

Muslim activism, not contemporary mainstream Islam. As Muslim writer Abdulaziz Sachedina maintains, the majority of Muslims embrace religious tolerance and human rights: "Most Muslims, like other human beings, are engaged in their day-to-day life in this world, struggling to provide for their . . . families, working for peaceful resolution to the conflicts that face them, and committed to honor universal human values of freedom and peace with justice." Moreover, most Muslims define jihad as a personal spiritual struggle, not as war or terrorism. In the opinion of U.S. Defense Secretary Donald Rumsfeld, terrorist networks such as al-Qaeda are attempting to "hijack" Islam. In response, he contends, "Muslims . . . are going to have to take back their religion and must not allow people to pervert it the way the al-Qaeda leadership is perverting it."

In the following chapter, commentators explore the question of whether the September 11 terrorist attack was motivated by Islamic beliefs, political extremism, or religious fundamentalism. Possible contributing factors, such as lax immigration standards and unintentional consequences of U.S. intelligence operations, are also examined.

Islamic Beliefs Led to the Attack on America

by Don Feder

About the author: *Don Feder, a nationally syndicated columnist, is the author of* Who's Afraid of the Religious Right? *and* A Jewish Conservative Looks at Pagan America.

On Oct. 7, 2001, the United States began bombing military installations and terrorist training camps in Afghanistan to avenge those who died in the attacks on the World Trade Center and the Pentagon. To call them victims of terrorism is too narrow a focus. In fact, they fell in the course of a world war—whose other casualties include Jews, Hindus, Orthodox Serbs and Indonesian Christians.

It's hard for ordinary Americans to understand the nature of the struggle when our leaders cling to a Disney version of Islam. President George W. Bush assures us that "the terrorists practice a fringe form of Islamic extremism . . . that perverts the peaceful teaching of Islam." If so, a large part of the Islamic world has perverted these peaceful teachings to such an extent that one wonders if the so-called deviation isn't actually the norm.

A more realistic perspective than the president's was offered by historian Paul Johnson, who wrote in the Oct. 15, 2001, issue of the *National Review* that "attacking terrorism at its roots necessarily involves conflict with the second-largest religious community in the world."

Resurgent Islam

From its seventh-century breakout from the Arabian peninsula until the late 17th century, Islam advanced at sword point, spreading from the Pyrenees to the Philippines. The tide was checked only at the gates of Vienna. From the decline of the Ottoman Empire until the 1970s, Islam ebbed. Today—fueled by oil wealth, surplus population, immigration and the rise of fundamentalism—Islam is resurgent. Instead of wild horsemen, its banners are carried by guerrillas, terrorists, theocrats and tyrants.

From "Q: Should Policymakers See Islam as an Enemy of the West? Yes: Islam Opposes Western Ideals Such as Tolerance, Democracy, and Civil Liberties," by Don Feder, *Insight on the News*, November 5, 2001. Copyright © 2001 by News World Communications, Inc. Reprinted with permission.

Chapter 1

A two-day conference in Rome in early October 2001 was intended to promote Christian-Muslim solidarity. But no sooner had it begun than Muslim clerics who were present were denouncing "arrogant Zionists." Yusuf al-Qaradawi, director of the influential Sunni Research Center in Qatar, said Muslims "refuse terrorism but don't consider it terrorism to defend one's own home."

In the year 2000, al-Qaradawi issued a *fatwa* decreeing that for Palestinians to stop committing atrocities

> *"If Islam is so mellow, why are the most contemptible crimes regularly committed in its name?"*

such as the attack on a Jerusalem pizzeria (where the detonation of a bomb packed with nails shredded the flesh of toddlers) would be "a religious sin and a betrayal of the nation." And al-Qaradawi is considered a moderate.

Imagine prominent Christian clerics debating the "morality" of Timothy McVeigh's mass murder in Oklahoma City. Well, just such a discussion has been going on among Islamic authorities regarding suicide attacks against Israelis.

The mufti of Saudi Arabia says that since the Koran forbids self-destruction, suicide bombings are impermissible, though the deaths of infidels in these attacks doesn't trouble the mufti. But Sheik Muhammad Sayyed Tantawi, a religious leader of Egypt's Sunni establishment, claims that taking one's own life in the process of killing the enemies of Islam isn't suicide but "self-defense and a kind of martyrdom."

Benign Islamic Beliefs?

If Islam is so mellow, why are the most contemptible crimes regularly committed in its name? There is no United Methodist Jihad. Suicide bombers don't quote the Book of Mormon. Individuals aren't given the choice of conversion to Judaism or death.

The day before the tallest buildings in Manhattan were reduced to rubble, this jihad caused blood to flow in the streets of Jos, a Nigerian city of 4 million. During 2001, thousands have died while fighting the attempts of Nigeria's northern states to impose Islamic law, including floggings, on nonbelievers.

In Indonesia, the Laskar Jihad has engaged in a campaign of religious cleansing in the Molucca islands, where as many as 5,000 Christians forcibly have been converted to Islam and the women subjected to genital mutilation in the process. On Oct. 1, 2001, a suicide squad blew up the legislative-assembly building in the Indian province of Kashmir (also targeted for conquest), killing 26 people. The Pakistan-based Army of the Prophet Muhammad—there they go again, distorting Islam's benign teachings—took responsibility.

There is an arc of conflict stretching from the west coast of Africa to the Philippines. Wherever sectarian violence rages, Muslims are pitted against non-Muslims. Sudan's Islamic regime has killed more than 2 million Christians and animists and revived the slave trade to dispose of captured women and children.

The objective is to convert or exterminate the nation's infidels.

A world away, the Abu Sayyaf rebels seek to create a Muslim state in Mindanao, an island with 35 percent of the Philippine land mass. Russian President Vladimir Putin has offered to share intelligence with the United States and has toned down his criticism of NATO expansion. In a recent trip to Europe, he talked about increasing oil and gas shipments to the West, to reduce dependence on Arab supplies.

Russia still is fighting Muslim separatists in Chechnya. In the year 2000, terrorist bombs exploded in Moscow and elsewhere in the federation (nearly 300 died). Putin may resent Russia's loss of empire, but when the chips are down he understands that the survival of Orthodox Russia lies with the West.

Attacks Against Other Religions

In addition to human casualties, Islam's war involves attacks on sacred symbols of other faiths. In the year 2000, Palestinians destroyed the Tomb of Rachel, which is one of Judaism's holiest sites. An American-born rabbi who rushed into the flames to save the Torah scrolls was murdered. A mosque was raised where the shrine's synagogue once stood.

Throughout the Middle East, thousands of churches have been demolished and replaced by mosques over the centuries. A mosque under construction in Nazareth is intended to overshadow the churches of Jesus' boyhood home. Under the Palestinian Authority, Bethlehem's Christians have dwindled from 80 percent to 20 percent of the city's population.

> *"Platitudes about terrorists perverting peaceful Islam only obscure a harsh reality."*

When Jordan controlled the Old City of Jerusalem, 58 synagogues were razed and Jewish cemeteries desecrated. Since NATO turned Kosovo over to Albanian Muslims, hundreds of Orthodox churches and monasteries have suffered a similar fate.

The Taliban's outrageous Buddha bashing should be seen in this light. It's not enough to subjugate, and in many cases, exterminate unbelievers. Any evidence that there once was another religion on Islamic soil must be effaced.

Some Guidelines

Guiding principles for policymakers include the following . . . :

• *Don't try to fight terrorism at the expense of those targeted by rogue states.* The United States is courting Sudan. Pakistan suddenly is an ally. But Sudan is waging total war on the nation's Christians. Kashmiri terrorists are trained in Pakistan. By advancing adversaries and undercutting real friends, we buy ourselves more trouble in the long run. . . .

• *See the interconnectedness of the struggle.* A story in *Newsweek* ("A Spreading Islamic Fire," Feb. 19, 2000) observed: "In the West Bank, in devastated

Chechnya and embattled Kashmir, in parts of Indonesia and the Philippines, . . . Islamist extremists are on the move and in contact with each other."

Osama bin Laden has his tentacles in Bosnia, Kosovo, Chechnya and the Philippines. Northern Nigeria's move to implement Sharia is funded by Saudi Arabia. Indonesia's Laskar Jihad includes veterans of fighting in Afghanistan and Bosnia. According to an Oct. 22, 2000, article in *The Guardian*, British Muslims were being trained in camps in the United Kingdom and sent to Lebanon and Jordan to join the holy war against Israel.

• *Tighten immigration.* Before the province was wrested from Yugoslavia, Muslims became a majority in Kosovo through massive illegal immigration from Albania. There are 5 million Muslims in France and more mosques than churches in the nation's south. Bologna's Cardinal Biffi urges Italy to favor Roman Catholic immigrants over Muslims to "save the nation's identity" from "Islam's ideological attack."

Islam now is the fastest-growing religion in the United States (an estimated 7 million followers). While many of these people are peaceful—and some may have left the Arab world to escape sectarian strife—immigrant communities contain terrorist cheering squads. When the imam at New York City's Hazrat-I-Abubakr Sadiq mosque denounced the World Trade Center attack, half of the congregation walked out. Is it wise for the West to import a potential fifth column?

Doubtless, the above will be decried as fear-mongering and intolerant. But tolerance is a Western concept that—along with democracy and civil liberties—does not exist in the Islamic world. Unlike communism during the Soviet twilight, there are millions—perhaps hundreds of millions—across the globe who are willing to die and kill for this creed. Platitudes about terrorists perverting peaceful Islam only obscure a harsh reality.

Political Extremism Led to the Attack on America

by Sohail Hashmi

About the author: *Sohail Hashmi teaches international relations at Mount Holyoke College in South Hadley, Massachusetts.*

The men who perpetrated the carnage on September 11, 2001, left a trail of clues about how they accomplished their mission, but virtually nothing about why. They left behind no suicide notes explaining what motivated them to kill thousands and die in the process, only the vaguest exhortations to be steadfast in the quest of paradise. But if they were indeed inspired by Osama bin Laden and his supporters, as the Bush administration promises to demonstrate, then they probably died for no more than an idea, the idea of *jihad*.

This term invokes for many in the West the notion of a holy war conducted by zealots in the name of their God with the aim of imposing their beliefs on recalcitrant unbelievers. Since September 11, we have heard this idea repeated by public officials. In his address to Congress, President George W. Bush described the goal of al Qaeda as "remaking the world and imposing its radical beliefs on people everywhere."

Yet it would be a mistake to view the attacks on the Pentagon and the World Trade Center as the latest phase of an Islamic holy war to convert or subjugate unbelievers. Based on the most illuminating of the few available statements of its mission, al Qaeda's goals appear to be far more mundane than religious, more political than theological. What's more, the organization's tactics bore all the characteristics of a guerilla attack, in which the infiltrators blended into the society they were attempting to terrorize, including, we are told, some of them spending one of their last nights drinking in a bar—hardly what could be expected of holy warriors.

Bin Laden's Grievances

The stated grievances of the bin Laden network fit a pattern familiar to students of Islamic activism over the past two centuries. In a *fatwa* released in

February 1998 (and echoed by the Taliban), bin Laden and leaders of extremist groups in Egypt, Pakistan and Bangladesh specified that their war was a defensive struggle against Americans and their allies who had declared war "on God, his messenger, and Muslims."

The "crimes and sins" perpetrated by the United States were threefold. First, it had "stormed" the Arabian peninsula during the Gulf War and continued "occupying the lands of Islam in the holiest of places" (i.e., Mecca and Medina in Saudi Arabia); second, it continued a war of annihilation against Iraq; and third, it supported the state of Israel and its continued occupation of Jerusalem.

> *"It would be a mistake to view the attacks on the Pentagon and the World Trade Center as the latest phase of an Islamic holy war to convert or subjugate unbelievers."*

The only appropriate Muslim response, according to the statement, was a defensive jihad to repulse the aggressor. According to virtually all classical and modern scholars, such a war—unlike the expansionist jihad—is a moral obligation incumbent upon all true Muslims.

This list of grievances is certainly not unique to bin Laden's group. The general complaint that the West is attacking Muslim countries has been heard repeatedly before, as has the goal of fighting the aggressors to compel their "armies to move out of all the lands of Islam, defeated and unable to threaten any Muslim."

The notion of jihad involved here is not the one formed during the period of Arab expansion in the 7th century or the Ottoman Turkish expansion of the 15th and 16th centuries, but the one formed over the past two centuries as Muslims struggled to respond to the expansion of the West. In the 19th and early 20th centuries, the aggressor nations would have been the British, the French, the Russians. Since the end of World War II, the United States has increasingly occupied this position, and all the more so after it became the guardian of the Persian Gulf during the late 1980s and '90s.

The fact that American support of Israel comes third on the list should not diminish its importance, as defenders of Israel have assiduously claimed in the weeks following September 11. The widespread perceptions that the United States provides carte blanche support to Israel even as the Jewish state occupies Jerusalem and large tracts of the West Bank and Gaza, that American-made weapons are used to kill Palestinians opposing the occupation—all while the sanctions against Iraq remain in place 10 years after the Gulf War—spark the rawest emotional responses. These complaints require no elaboration in the fatwa; they are immediately understood by the statement's intended Muslim audience.

If we accept the fatwa as articulating the ideas that drive bin Laden and his supporters, then there is nothing at all remarkable about his group. They selectively quote from the Koran to establish the basis for their jihad, but their motivations appear to spring primarily from the same sort of anti-imperialism that motivates religious and non-religious groups in the Middle East and other parts of the world. They may view themselves as the vanguard of an ideological movement that will ultimately overturn the societies of the rich and powerful West, but their words and actions indicate they are astute enough to realize this is a remote possibility.

Although they sometimes appear to be fired by the religious zeal of the puritanical Wahhabi movements that twice swept Arabia, their targets to date have not been offending religious or cultural institutions, but political, military and economic targets: American embassies in Africa, military barracks in Saudi Arabia, the USS *Cole*, the Pentagon and the World Trade Center. Moreover, the

> *"Muslim scholars have for centuries rejected indiscriminate killing and the terrorizing of civilian populations as a legitimate form of jihad."*

long-term planning and coordination required for the September 11 attacks demonstrate that al Qaeda is a far cry from Hamas and Islamic Jihad in the Palestinian territories. Whereas the Palestinian suicide bombers are recruited from mosques or the street just days or hours before they die, the attacks in the United States required years of planning.

Most people, including many Arabs and Muslims, probably consider bin Laden's avowed goal of driving the United States out of the Middle East to be impractical and even imprudent. Still, many people of good faith, Muslims and non-Muslims, Americans and non-Americans, may share the general concerns with U.S. policies in the region that al Qaeda has outlined as the basis for its jihad.

Not Everything Is Permissible in Jihad

It is when we cross from motivations to methods that people of good faith— and especially Muslims—must unequivocally part company with the extremists. We cannot allow them to say, in pursuing their idea, that everything is permissible. The thrust of the entire jihad tradition to which they appeal makes it clear that everything is not permissible.

No principle is more clearly outlined in the Koran than this, that even in the midst of battle—a realm of human activity where moral constraints are often loosened—constraints must be maintained. In one of the first verses outlining a military aspect to jihad, the injunction is clear: "Fight in the cause of God those who fight you, but do not transgress limits, for God loves not the transgressor" (2:190). Commenting on this verse, the prominent Syrian scholar Wahba Zuhayli writes: "Do not fight anyone unless they fight you. Fighting is thus justified if you fight the enemy and the enemy fights you. It is not justified against anyone who does not fight the Muslims, and it is necessary [in this event] to make peace." Zuhayli clearly rules out the possibility of collective responsibility—that all citizens belonging to a perceived foe are somehow responsible.

The presumption of Islamic teachings on right conduct in war is that individuals are innocent and therefore not subject to harm unless they demonstrate by their actions that they are a threat to the safety of Muslims. On this basis, the overwhelming majority of Muslim scholars have for centuries rejected indiscriminate killing and the terrorizing of civilian populations as a legitimate form of jihad.

Bin Laden and his supporters give a brutally simple response to the weight of the jihad tradition: "We do not differentiate between those dressed in military uniforms and civilians," he has said. Because "U.S. aggression is affecting Muslim civilians, not just the military," all Americans "are targets in this fatwa."

In the name of retaliation, they claim, there are no innocents.

This logic must also be rejected. It leads us into the infernal and morally vacuous exercise of assigning blame—a process of tit-for-tat that leads, ad infinitum, into the past and holds the potential for disastrous consequences in the future if the spiral is unbroken.

Religious Fundamentalism Led to the Attack on America

by Andrew Sullivan

About the author: *Andrew Sullivan is a senior editor of the weekly magazine the* New Republic.

Perhaps the most admirable part of the response to the conflict that began on September 11 has been a general reluctance to call it a religious war. Officials and commentators have rightly stressed that this is not a battle between the Muslim world and the West, that the murderers are not representative of Islam. President George W. Bush went to the Islamic Center in Washington to reinforce the point. At prayer meetings across the United States and throughout the world, Muslim leaders have been included alongside Christians, Jews and Buddhists.

The only problem with this otherwise laudable effort is that it doesn't hold up under inspection. The religious dimension of this conflict is central to its meaning. The words of Osama bin Laden are saturated with religious argument and theological language. Whatever else the Taliban regime is in Afghanistan, it is fanatically religious. Although some Muslim leaders have criticized the terrorists, and even Saudi Arabia's rulers have distanced themselves from the militants, other Muslims in the Middle East and elsewhere have not denounced these acts, have been conspicuously silent or have indeed celebrated them. The terrorists' strain of Islam is clearly not shared by most Muslims and is deeply unrepresentative of Islam's glorious, civilized and peaceful past. But it surely represents a part of Islam—a radical, fundamentalist part—that simply cannot be ignored or denied.

Religious Underpinnings

In that sense, this surely is a religious war—but not of Islam versus Christianity and Judaism. Rather, it is a war of fundamentalism against faiths of all kinds that are at peace with freedom and modernity. This war even has far gentler echoes in America's own religious conflicts—between newer, more virulent strands of Christian fundamentalism and mainstream Protestantism and Catholicism. These conflicts have ancient roots, but they seem to be gaining new force as modernity spreads and deepens. They are our new wars of religion—and their victims are in all likelihood going to mount with each passing year.

Osama bin Laden himself couldn't be clearer about the religious underpinnings of his campaign of terror. In 1998, he told his followers, "The call to wage war against America was made because America has spearheaded the crusade against the Islamic nation, sending tens of thousands of its troops to the land of the two holy mosques over and above its meddling in its affairs and its politics and its support of the oppressive, corrupt and tyrannical regime that is in control." Notice the use of the word "crusade," an explicitly religious term, and one that simply ignores the fact that the last few major American interventions abroad—in Kuwait, Somalia and the Balkans—were all conducted in defense of Muslims.

> *"The terrorists' strain of Islam is clearly not shared by most Muslims. . . . But it surely represents a part of Islam . . . that simply cannot be ignored or denied."*

Notice also that as bin Laden understands it, the "crusade" America is alleged to be leading is not against Arabs but against the Islamic nation, which spans many ethnicities. This nation knows no nation-states as they actually exist in the region—which is why this form of Islamic fundamentalism is also so worrying to the rulers of many Middle Eastern states. Notice also that bin Laden's beef is with American troops defiling the land of Saudi Arabia—"the land of the two holy mosques," in Mecca and Medina. In 1998, he also told followers that his terrorism was "of the commendable kind, for it is directed at the tyrants and the aggressors and the enemies of Allah." He has a litany of grievances against Israel as well, but his concerns are not primarily territorial or procedural. "Our religion is under attack," he said baldly. The attackers are Christians and Jews. When asked to sum up his message to the people of the West, bin Laden couldn't have been clearer: "Our call is the call of Islam that was revealed to Muhammad. It is a call to all mankind. We have been entrusted with good cause to follow in the footsteps of the messenger and to communicate his message to all nations."

A Violent Strain in Islam

This is a religious war against "unbelief and unbelievers," in bin Laden's words. Are these cynical words designed merely to use Islam for nefarious ends? We cannot know the precise motives of bin Laden, but we can know that he would not use these words if he did not think they had salience among the people he wishes to inspire and provoke. This form of Islam is not restricted to bin Laden alone.

Its roots lie in an extreme and violent strain in Islam that emerged in the 18th century in opposition to what was seen by some Muslims as Ottoman decadence but has gained greater strength in the 20th. For the past two decades, this form of Islamic fundamentalism has racked the Middle East. It has targeted almost every regime in the region and, as it failed to make progress, has extended its hostility into the West. From the assassination of Anwar Sadat to the fatwa against Salman Rushdie to the decade-long campaign of bin Laden to the destruction of ancient Buddhist statues and the hideous persecution of women and homosexuals by the Taliban to the World Trade Center massacre, there is a single line. That line is a fundamentalist, religious one. And it is an Islamic one.

Most interpreters of the Koran find no arguments in it for the murder of innocents. But it would be naive to ignore in Islam a deep thread of intolerance toward unbelievers, especially if those unbelievers are believed to be a threat to the Islamic world. There are many passages in the Koran urging mercy toward others, tolerance, respect for life and so on. But there are also passages as violent as this: "And when the sacred months are passed, kill those who join other gods with God wherever ye shall find them; and seize them, besiege them, and lay wait for them with every kind of ambush." And this: "Believers! Wage war against such of the infidels as are your neighbors, and let them find you rigorous." Bernard Lewis,

> *"[This] is a war of fundamentalism against faiths of all kinds that are at peace with freedom and modernity."*

the great scholar of Islam, writes of the dissonance within Islam: "There is something in the religious culture of Islam which inspired, in even the humblest peasant or peddler, a dignity and a courtesy toward others never exceeded and rarely equaled in other civilizations. And yet, in moments of upheaval and disruption, when the deeper passions are stirred, this dignity and courtesy toward others can give way to an explosive mixture of rage and hatred which impels even the government of an ancient and civilized country—even the spokesman of a great spiritual and ethical religion—to espouse kidnapping and assassination, and try to find, in the life of their prophet, approval and indeed precedent for such actions." Since Muhammad was, unlike many other religious leaders, not simply a sage or a prophet but a ruler in his own right, this exploitation of his politics is not as great a stretch as some would argue.

This use of religion for extreme repression, and even terror, is not of course restricted to Islam. For most of its history, Christianity has had a worse record. From the Crusades to the Inquisition to the bloody religious wars of the 16th and 17th centuries, Europe saw far more blood spilled for religion's sake than the Muslim world did. And given how expressly nonviolent the teachings of the Gospels are, the perversion of Christianity in this respect was arguably greater than bin Laden's selective use of Islam. But it is there nonetheless. It seems almost as if there is something inherent in religious monotheism that lends itself to this kind of terrorist temptation. And our bland attempts to ignore this—to speak of this violence as if it did not have religious roots—is some kind of denial. We don't want to denigrate religion as such, and so we deny that religion is at the heart of this. But we would understand this conflict better, perhaps, if we first acknowledged that religion is responsible in some way, and then figured out how and why.

The Voice of Fundamentalism

The first mistake is surely to condescend to fundamentalism. We may disagree with it, but it has attracted millions of adherents for centuries, and for a good reason. It elevates and comforts. It provides a sense of meaning and direction to those lost in a disorienting world. The blind recourse to texts embraced as literal truth, the injunction to follow the commandments of God before anything else, the subjugation of reason and judgment and even conscience to the dictates of dogma: these can be exhilarating and transformative. They have led human beings to perform extraordinary acts of both good and evil. And they have an internal logic to them. If you believe that there is an eternal afterlife and that endless indescribable torture awaits those who disobey God's law, then it requires no huge stretch of imagination to make sure that you not only conform to each diktat but that you also encourage and, if necessary, coerce others to do the same. The logic behind this is impeccable. Sin begets sin. The sin of others can corrupt you as well. The only solution is to construct a world in which such sin is outlawed and punished and constantly purged—by force if necessary. It is not crazy to act this way if you believe these things strongly enough. In some ways, it's crazier to believe these things and not act this way.

In a world of absolute truth, in matters graver than life and death, there is no room for dissent and no room for theological doubt. Hence the reliance on literal interpretations of texts—because interpretation can lead to error, and error can lead to damnation. Hence also the ancient Catholic insistence on absolute church authority. Without infallibility, there can be no guarantee of truth. Without such a guarantee, confusion can lead to hell.

Russian novelist Fyodor Dostoyevsky's Grand Inquisitor makes the case perhaps as well as anyone. In the story told by Ivan Karamazov in "The Brothers Karamazov," Jesus returns to earth during the Spanish Inquisition. On a day when hundreds have been burned at the stake for heresy, Jesus performs miracles. Alarmed, the Inquisitor arrests Jesus and imprisons him with the intent of burning him at the stake as well. What follows is a conversation between the Inquisitor and Jesus. Except it isn't a conversation because Jesus says nothing. It is really a dialogue between two modes of religion, an exploration of the tension between the extraordinary, transcendent claims of religion and human beings' inability to live up to them, or even fully believe them.

According to the Inquisitor, Jesus' crime was revealing that salvation was possible but still allowing humans the freedom to refuse it. And this, to the Inquisitor, was a form of cruelty. When the truth involves the most important things imaginable—the meaning of life, the fate of one's eternal soul, the difference between good and evil—it is not enough to premise it on the capacity of human choice. That is too great a burden. Choice leads to unbelief or distraction or negligence or despair. What human beings really need is the certainty of truth, and they need to see it reflected in everything around them—in the cultures in which they live, enveloping them in a seamless fabric of faith that helps them resist the terror of choice and the abyss of unbelief. This need is what the In-

> *"It would be naive to ignore in Islam a deep thread of intolerance toward unbelievers."*

quisitor calls the "fundamental secret of human nature." He explains: "These pitiful creatures are concerned not only to find what one or the other can worship, but to find something that all would believe in and worship; what is essential is that all may be together in it. This craving for community of worship is the chief misery of every man individually and of all humanity since the beginning of time."

This is the voice of fundamentalism. Faith cannot exist alone in a single person. Indeed, faith needs others for it to survive—and the more complete the culture of faith, the wider it is, and the more total its infiltration of the world, the better. It is hard for us to wrap our minds around this today, but it is quite clear from the accounts of the Inquisition and, indeed, of the religious wars that continued to rage in Europe for nearly three centuries, that many of the fanatics who burned human beings at the stake were acting out of what they genuinely thought were the best interests of the victims. With the power of the state, they used fire, as opposed to simple execution, because it was thought to be spiritually cleansing. A few minutes of hideous torture on earth were deemed a small price to pay for helping such souls avoid eternal torture in the afterlife. Moreover, the example of such government-sponsored executions helped create a culture in which certain truths were reinforced and in which it was easier for more weak people to find faith. The burden of this duty to uphold the faith lay on the men required to torture, persecute and murder the unfaithful. And many of them believed, as no doubt some Islamic fundamentalists believe, that they were acting out of mercy and godliness.

This is the authentic voice of the Taliban. It also finds itself replicated in secular form. What, after all, were the totalitarian societies of Nazi Germany or Soviet Russia if not an exact replica of this kind of fusion of politics and ultimate meaning? Under Lenin's and Stalin's rules, the imminence of salvation through revolutionary consciousness was in perpetual danger of being undermined by those too weak to have faith—the bourgeois or the kulaks or the intellectuals. So they had to be liquidated or purged. Similarly, it is easy for us to dismiss the Nazis as evil, as they surely were. It is harder for us to understand that in some twisted fashion, they truly believed that they were creating a new dawn for humanity, a place where all the doubts that freedom brings could be dispelled in a rapture of racial purity and destiny. Hence the destruction of all dissidents and the Jews—carried out by fire as the Inquisitors had before, an act of purification different merely in its scale, efficiency and Godlessness.

The Logic of Fundamentalist Terrorism

Perhaps the most important thing for us to realize today is that the defeat of each of these fundamentalisms required a long and arduous effort. The conflict with Islamic fundamentalism is likely to take as long. For unlike Europe's religious wars, which taught Christians the futility of fighting to the death over something beyond human understanding and so immune to any definitive resolution, there has been no such educative conflict in the Muslim world. Only Iran and Afghanistan have experienced the full horror of revolutionary fundamentalism, and only Iran has so far seen reason to moderate to some extent. From everything we see, the lessons Europe learned in its bloody history have yet to be absorbed within the Muslim world. There, as in 16th-century Europe, the promise of purity and salvation seems far more enticing than the mundane allure of mere peace. That means that we are not at the end of this conflict but in its very early stages.

America is not a neophyte in this struggle. The United States has seen several waves of religious fervor since its founding. But American evangelicalism has always kept its distance from governmental power. The Christian separation between what is God's and what is Caesar's—drawn from the Gospels—helped restrain the fundamentalist temptation. The last few decades have proved an exception, however. As modernity advanced, and the certitudes of fundamentalist faith seemed mocked by an increasingly liberal society, evangelicals mobilized and entered politics. Their faith sharpened, their zeal intensified, the temptation to fuse political and religious authority beckoned more insistently.

> *"There is something inherent in religious monotheism that lends itself to . . . [the] terrorist temptation."*

Mercifully, violence has not been a significant feature of this trend—but it has not been absent. The murders of abortion providers show what such zeal can lead to. And indeed, if people truly believe that abortion is the same as mass murder, then you can see the awful logic of the terrorism it has spawned. This is the same logic as bin Laden's. If faith is that strong, and it dictates a choice between action or eternal damnation, then violence can easily be justified. In retrospect, we should be amazed not that violence has occurred—but that it hasn't occurred more often.

The critical link between Western and Middle Eastern fundamentalism is surely the pace of social change. If you take your beliefs from books written more than a thousand years ago, and you believe in these texts literally, then the appearance of the modern world must truly terrify. If you believe that women should be consigned to polygamous, concealed servitude, then Manhattan must appear like Gomorrah. If you believe that homosexuality is a crime punishable by death, as both fundamentalist Islam and the Bible dictate, then a world of same-sex marriage is surely Sodom. It is not a big step to argue that such centers of evil should be destroyed or undermined, as bin Laden does, or to believe that their destruction is somehow a consequence of their sin, as Christian fundamentalist Jerry Falwell argued. Look again at Falwell's now infamous words in the wake of September 11: "I really believe that the pagans, and the abortionists, and the feminists, and the gays and lesbians who are actively trying to make that an alternative lifestyle, the A.C.L.U., People for the American Way— all of them who have tried to secularize America—I point the finger in their face and say, 'You helped this happen.'"

And why wouldn't he believe that? He has subsequently apologized for the insensitivity of the remark but not for its theological underpinning. He cannot repudiate the theology—because it is the essence of what he believes in and must believe in for his faith to remain alive.

The Threat of Insecurity

The other critical aspect of this kind of faith is insecurity. American fundamentalists know they are losing the culture war. They are terrified of failure and of the Godless world they believe is about to engulf or crush them. They speak and think defensively. They talk about renewal, but in their private discourse they expect damnation for an America that has lost sight of the fundamentalist notion of God.

Similarly, Muslims know that the era of Islam's imperial triumph has long since gone. For many centuries, the civilization of Islam was the center of the world. It eclipsed Europe in the Dark Ages, fostered great learning and expanded territorially well into Europe and Asia. But it has all been downhill from there. From the collapse of the Ottoman Empire onward, it has been on the losing side of history. The response to this has been an intermittent flirtation with Westernization but far more emphatically a reaffirmation of the most irredentist and extreme forms of the culture under threat. Hence the odd phenomenon of Islamic extremism beginning in earnest only in the last 200 years.

With Islam, this has worse implications than for other cultures that have had rises and falls. For Islam's religious tolerance has always been premised on its own power. It was tolerant when it controlled the territory and called the shots. When it lost territory and saw itself eclipsed by the West in power and civilization, tolerance evaporated. To cite Lewis again on Islam: "What is truly evil and unacceptable is the domination of infidels over true believers. For true believers to rule misbelievers is proper and natural, since this provides for the maintenance of the holy law and gives the misbelievers both the opportunity and the incentive to embrace the true faith. But for misbelievers to rule over true believers is blasphemous and unnatural, since it leads to the corruption of religion and morality in society and to the flouting or even the abrogation of God's law."

"If faith . . . dictates a choice between action or eternal damnation, then violence can easily be justified."

Thus the horror at the establishment of the State of Israel, an infidel country in Muslim lands, a bitter reminder of the eclipse of Islam in the modern world. Thus also the revulsion at American bases in Saudi Arabia. While colonialism of different degrees is merely political oppression for some cultures, for Islam it was far worse. It was blasphemy that had to be avenged and countered.

Acting Out Internal Conflict

I cannot help thinking of this defensiveness when I read stories of the suicide bombers sitting poolside in Florida or racking up a $48 vodka tab in an American restaurant. We tend to think that this assimilation into the West might bring Islamic fundamentalists around somewhat, temper their zeal. But in fact, the opposite is the case. The temptation of American and Western culture—indeed, the very allure of such culture—may well require a repression all the more brutal if it is to be overcome. The transmission of American culture into the heart of what bin Laden calls the Islamic nation requires only two responses—capitulation to unbelief or a radical strike against it. There is little room in the fundamentalist psyche for a moderate accommodation. The very psychological dynamics that lead repressed homosexuals to be viciously homophobic or that entice sexually tempted preachers to inveigh against immorality are the very dynamics that lead vodka-drinking fundamentalists to steer planes into buildings. It is not designed to achieve anything, construct anything, argue anything. It is a violent acting out of internal conflict.

And America is the perfect arena for such acting out. For the question of religious fundamentalism was not only familiar to the founding fathers. In many ways, it was the central question that led to America's existence. The first American immigrants, after all, were refugees from the religious wars that engulfed England and that intensified under England's Taliban, Oliver Cromwell. One central influence on the founders' political thought was John Locke, the English liberal who wrote the now famous "Letter on Toleration." In it, Locke argued that true salvation could not be a result of coercion, that faith had to be freely chosen to be genuine and that any other interpretation was counter to the Gospels. Following Locke, the founders established as a central element of the new American order a stark separation of church and state, ensuring that no single religion could use political means to enforce its own orthodoxies.

We cite this as a platitude today without absorbing or even realizing its radical nature in human history—and the deep human predicament it was designed to solve. It was an attempt to answer the eternal human question of how to pursue the goal of religious salvation for ourselves and others and yet also maintain civil peace. What the founders and Locke were saying was that the ultimate claims of religion should simply not be allowed to interfere with political and religious freedom. They did this to preserve peace above all—but also to preserve true religion itself.

The Importance of Church-State Separation

The security against an American Taliban is therefore relatively simple: it's the Constitution. And the surprising consequence of this separation is not that it led to a collapse of religious faith in America—as weak human beings found themselves unable to believe without social and political reinforcement—but that it led to one of the most vibrantly religious civil societies on earth. No other country has achieved this. And it is this achievement that the Taliban and bin Laden have now decided to challenge. It is a living, tangible rebuke to everything they believe in.

That is why this coming conflict is indeed as momentous and as grave as the last major conflicts, against Nazism and Communism, and why it is not hyperbole to see it in these epic terms. What is at stake is yet another battle against a religion that is succumbing to the temptation Jesus refused in the desert—to rule by force. The difference is that this conflict is against a more formidable enemy than Nazism or Communism. The secular totalitarianisms of the 20th century were, in President Bush's memorable words, "discarded lies." They were fundamentalisms built on the very weak intellectual conceits of a master race and a Communist revolution.

But Islamic fundamentalism is based on a glorious civilization and a great faith. It can harness and co-opt and corrupt true and good believers if it has a propitious and toxic enough environment. It has a more powerful logic than either Stalin's or Hitler's Godless ideology, and it can serve as a focal point for all the other societies in the world, whose resentment of Western success and civilization comes more easily than the arduous

> *"We are fighting for religion against one of the deepest strains in religion there is. And not only our lives but our souls are at stake."*

task of accommodation to modernity. We have to somehow defeat this without defeating or even opposing a great religion that is nonetheless extremely inexperienced in the toleration of other ascendant and more powerful faiths. It is hard to underestimate the extreme delicacy and difficulty of this task.

In this sense, the symbol of this conflict should not be Old Glory, however stirring it is. What is really at issue here is the simple but immensely difficult principle of the separation of politics and religion. We are fighting not for our country as such or for our flag. We are fighting for the universal principles of our Constitution—and the possibility of free religious faith it guarantees. We are fighting for religion against one of the deepest strains in religion there is. And not only our lives but our souls are at stake.

Western Leftism Contributed to the Attack on America

by Waller R. Newell

About the author: *Waller R. Newell is professor of political science and philosophy at Carleton University in Ottawa, Canada.*

Much has been written about Osama bin Laden's Islamic fundamentalism; less about the contribution of European Marxist postmodernism to bin Laden's thinking. In fact, the ideology by which al Qaeda justifies its acts of terror owes as much to baleful trends in Western thought as it does to a perversion of Muslim beliefs. Osama's doctrine of terror is partly a Western export.

To see this, it is necessary to revisit the intellectual brew that produced the ideology of Third World socialism in the 1960s. A key figure here is the German philosopher Martin Heidegger (1889–1976), who not only helped shape several generations of European leftists and founded postmodernism, but also was a leading supporter of the Nazis. Heidegger argued for the primacy of "peoples" in contrast with the alienating individualism of "modernity." In order to escape the yoke of Western capitalism and the "idle chatter" of constitutional democracy, the "people" would have to return to its primordial destiny through an act of violent revolutionary "resolve."

A Self-Sacrificing Collectivism

Heidegger saw in the Nazis just this return to the blood-and-soil heritage of the authentic German people. Paradoxically, the Nazis embraced technology at its most advanced to shatter the iron cage of modernity and bring back the purity of the distant past. And they embraced terror and violence to push beyond the modern present—hence the term "postmodern"—and vault the people back before modernity, with its individual liberties and market economy, to the imagined collective austerity of the feudal age.

This vision of the postmodernist revolution went straight from Heidegger into the French postwar Left, especially the works of Jean-Paul Sartre, eager apologist for Stalinism and the Cultural Revolution in China. Sartre's protégé, the Algerian writer Frantz Fanon, crystallized the Third World variant of postmodernist revolution in *The Wretched of the Earth* (1961). From there, it entered the world of Middle Eastern radicals. Many of the leaders of the Islamic Shiite revolution in Iran that deposed the modernizing shah and brought the Ayatollah Khomeini to power in 1979 had studied Fanon's brand of Marxism. Ali Shari'at, the Sorbonne-educated Iranian sociologist of religion considered by many the intellectual father of the Shiite revolution, translated *The Wretched of the Earth* and Sartre's *Being and Nothingness* into Persian. The Iranian revolution was a synthesis of Islamic fundamentalism and European Third World socialism.

In the postmodernist leftism of these revolutionaries, the "people" supplanted Marx's proletariat as the agent of revolution. Following Heidegger and Fanon, leaders like Lin Piao, ideologist of the Red Guards in China, and Pol Pot, student of leftist philosophy in France before becoming a founder of the Khmer Rouge in Cambodia, justified revolution as a therapeutic act by which non-Western peoples would regain the dignity they had lost to colonial oppressors and to American-style materialism, selfishness, and immorality. A purifying violence would purge the people of egoism and hedonism and draw them back into a primitive collective of self-sacrifice.

Marxism and Islamic Revolution

Many elements in the ideology of al Qaeda—set forth most clearly in Osama bin Laden's 1996 "Declaration of War Against America"—derive from this same mix. Indeed, in Arab intellectual circles today, bin Laden is already being likened to an earlier icon of Third World revolution who renounced a life of privilege to head for the mountains and fight the American oppressor, Che Guevara. According to Cairo journalist Issandr Elamsani, Arab leftist intellectuals still see the world very much in 1960s terms. "They are all ex-Sorbonne, old Marxists," he says, "who look at everything through a postcolonial prism."

Just as Heidegger wanted the German people to return to a foggy, medieval, blood-and-soil collectivism purged of the corruptions of modernity, and just as Pol Pot wanted Cambodia to return to the Year Zero, so does Osama dream of returning his world to the imagined purity of seventh-century Islam. And just as Fanon argued that revolution can never accomplish its

> *"The ideology by which al Qaeda justifies its acts of terror owes as much to baleful trends in Western thought as it does to a perversion of Muslim beliefs."*

goals through negotiation or peaceful reform, so does Osama regard terror as good in itself, a therapeutic act, quite apart from any concrete aim. The willingness to kill is proof of one's purity.

According to journalist Robert Worth, writing in the *New York Times* on the intellectual roots of Islamic terror, bin Laden is poorly educated in Islamic theology. A wealthy playboy in his youth, he fell under the influence of radical Arab intellectuals of the 1960s who blended calls for Marxist revolution with calls for a pure Islamic state.

> *"Just as [leftist writer Frantz] Fanon argued that revolution can never accomplish its goals through negotiation or peaceful reform, so does Osama regard terror as good in itself."*

Many of these men were imprisoned and executed for their attacks on Arab regimes; Sayyid Qutb, for example, a major figure in the rise of Islamic fundamentalism, was executed in Egypt in 1965. But their ideas lived on. Qutb's intellectual progeny included Fathi Yakan, who likened the coming Islamic revolution to the French and Russian revolutions, Abdullah Azzam, a Palestinian activist killed in a car bombing in 1989, and Safar Al-Hawali, a Saudi fundamentalist frequently jailed by the Saudi government. As such men dreamed of a pure Islamic state, European revolutionary ideology was seldom far from their minds. Wrote Fathi Yakan, "The groundwork for the French Revolution was laid by Rousseau, Voltaire and Montesquieu; the Communist Revolution realized plans set by Marx, Engels and Lenin. . . . The same holds true for us as well."

A Melding of Islamism and Socialism

The influence of Qutb's *Signposts on the Road* (1964) is clearly traceable in pronouncements by Islamic Jihad, the group that would justify its assassination of Egyptian president Anwar Sadat in 1981 as a step toward ending American domination of Egypt and ushering in a pure Islamic order. In the 1990s, Islamic Jihad would merge with al Qaeda, and Osama's "Declaration of War Against America" in turn would show an obvious debt to the Islamic Jihad manifesto "The Neglected Duty."

It can be argued, then, that the birthplace of Osama's brand of terrorism was Paris 1968, when, amid the student riots and radical teach-ins, the influence of Sartre, Fanon, and the new postmodernist Marxist champions of the "people's destiny" was at its peak. By the mid '70s, according to Claire Sterling's *The Terror Network*, "practically every terrorist and guerrilla force to speak of was represented in Paris. . . . The Palestinians especially were there in force." This was the heyday of Palestinian leader Yasser Arafat's terrorist organization Al Fatah, whose 1968 tract "The Revolution and Violence" has been called "a selective précis of *The Wretched of the Earth.*"

While Al Fatah occasionally still used the old-fashioned Leninist language of class struggle, the increasingly radical groups that succeeded it perfected the melding of Islamism and Third World socialism. Their tracts blended Heidegger and Fanon with calls to revive a strict Islamic social order. "We declare," says the Shiite terrorist group Hezbollah in its "Open Letter to the Downtrodden in Lebanon and the World" (1985), "that we are a nation that fears only God" and will not accept "humiliation from America and its allies and the Zionist entity that has usurped the sacred Islamic land." The aim of violent struggle is "giving all our people the opportunity to determine their fate." But that fate must follow the prescribed course: "We do not hide our commitment to the rule of Islam, . . . which alone guarantees justice and dignity for all and prevents any new imperialist attempt to infiltrate our country. . . . This Islamic resistance must . . . with God's help receive from all Muslims in all parts of the world utter support."

A Will Unrestrained by Morality

These 1980s calls to revolution could have been uttered in late 2001 by Osama bin Laden. Indeed, the chief doctrinal difference between the radicals of several decades ago and Osama only confirms the influence of postmodernist socialism on the latter: Whereas Qutb and other early Islamists looked mainly inward, concentrating on revolution in Muslim countries, Osama directs his struggle primarily outward, against American hegemony. While for the early revolutionaries, toppling their own tainted regimes was the principal path to the purified Islamic state, for Osama, the chief goal is bringing America to its knees. . . .

What the terrorists have in common with our [leftist] nihilists is a belief in the primacy of the radical will, unrestrained by traditional moral teachings such as the requirements of prudence, fairness, and reason. The terrorists seek to put this belief into action, shattering tradition through acts of violent revolutionary resolve. That is how al Qaeda can ignore mainstream Islam, which prohibits the deliberate killing of noncombatants, and slaughter innocents in the name of creating a new world, the latest in a long line of grimly punitive collectivist utopias.

Post–Cold War Lassitude Contributed to the Attack on America

by Gary Hart

About the author: *Gary Hart is a former Democratic senator from Colorado.*

Should the United States have foreseen the seriousness of the terrorist threat and the real possibility that major symbolic targets, such as the World Trade Center and the Pentagon, would be attacked by terrorists using commercial airliners as guided missiles? Were there warnings and, if so, why were they not taken seriously? Why were rare early signals of danger disregarded by policymakers and press alike? Most of all, what factors contributed to America's dazed entry into the new and newly dangerous 21st century?

Historians and concerned citizens will be pondering these questions for decades, perhaps centuries, to come.

As early as 15 September 1999, almost exactly two years before the attacks, the United States Commission on National Security/21st Century warned that terrorist attacks would occur on American soil, and that Americans would lose their lives, possibly in large numbers. Virtually no one listened in an America that was at peace, powerful and prosperous.

Why Did America Ignore the Warnings?

A confluence of factors contributed to America's lassitude.

First, America lost its coalescing cause. In the late 1980s, a prominent Soviet interlocutor characterised the emerging Gorbachev era as threatening to the US for this unpredictable reason: "We are about to take away your enemy." From George Kennan's admonition in 1946 that communism must be contained, until the fall of the Soviet empire in December 1991, the central organising principle for America and much of the west was the cold war effort to contain the spread of communism. The age was characterised by the Korean and Vietnam wars, together with the overthrow of unfriendly governments, support for friendly but often undemocratic governments, assassination plots against foreign leaders and countless covert operations.

But, in a veritable heartbeat, the cold war was over. Though US military spending would remain large, and defence structures would remain basically the same as during the cold war (albeit slightly smaller in scope and scale), those asked to do "net threat assessments" would be hard-pressed to identify an enemy. Some on the right struggled hard to find, in the People's Republic of China, a foe worthy of the all-out military/preparedness once warranted by the former Soviet Union. Less ideological military planners settled for a post–cold war force structure large enough for "two major theatre wars", namely Korea and the Persian Gulf. Those not persuaded by the idea of an expansionist China, or the restart of the Korean and Persian Gulf wars, focused instead on the need to resuscitate Reagan's Star Wars programme in the form of a national missile defence system against attacks from "rogue states".

> *"[A commission] warned that terrorist attacks would occur on American soil, and that Americans would lose their lives, possibly in large numbers."*

War itself, however, was being transformed from conflict between the massed armies of nation states to low-intensity urban conflict among tribes, clans and gangs.

While the superpowers locked horns, the second half of the 20th century saw traditional wars between nation states give way to wars of national liberation, principally carried out in Africa, Asia and Latin America against declining colonial powers. America faced unconventional, guerrilla warfare in Vietnam, as did the Soviet Union in Afghanistan. Mid-century guerrilla wars of national liberation against ageing colonial powers gradually migrated to terrorist clashes between ethnic and religious factions. Ethnic nationalism, religious fundamentalism and non-state actors began to emerge.

The state lost its monopoly on violence, and the distinction between war and crime quickly began to disappear. As the cold war wound down, the US stepped up its exportation of democracy, liberalism and capitalism to parts of the world—especially the Islamic crescent—that neither shared nor appreciated them.

Following the end of the Vietnam war, most Americans did not want to be bothered by complex, local, tribal conflicts that did not seem to threaten them. The US presence in places such as Somalia, Haiti, Kosovo and elsewhere seemed unproductive and unnecessary. Those military forces stationed abroad, in places as disparate as Beirut, Saudi Arabia and Yemen, soon became targets of fanatical terrorist organisations that did not respect traditional rules of war. Our decision to contain communism had taken us down this unfamiliar road.

Post–Cold War Excesses

The cold war toll in lives, national treasure and, occasionally, prestige was enormous. As could be expected at the close of any such extended national exertion, the successful conclusion of this effort at the beginning of the last decade of a violent 20th century led to an almost universal desire to replace collective vigilance with individual exuberance, and care with escape. Like the Roaring Twenties, the Nineties thus became a time when cautionary warnings of new dangers, necessarily vague and unfocused, would not resonate in a nation exhausted from the tensions of missile crises and "a long twilight struggle".

The age of acquisition quickly filled the vacuum created by the close of the cold war. During the decade following the collapse of the Soviet Union, America would be very much awake to new commercial possibilities—even as it refused to see the dangers created by a world shifting under its feet. America was transfixed for more than four decades by the threat of communism: its demise left America without its main organising principle. Containment of communism, so central to US planning throughout the second half of the 20th century, gave way to the enthusiasms and excesses of the dotcom bubble.

At the end of the 20th century, there was a confluence of a number of revolutions. The global economy, the information revolution, round-the-clock financial markets, instant communications and mass international travel all led to the triumph of technological capitalism and, at the same time, growing global divisions between the elite haves and the increasingly desperate have-nots. Resentment of the

"Following the end of the Vietnam war, most Americans did not want to be bothered by complex, local, tribal conflicts that did not seem to threaten them."

haves by the masses of have-nots, and resentment of exported American popular culture, escalated dangerously.

The United States, triumphant in the ideological and quasimilitary struggle with communism, continued to spend the 1990s exporting its values. These values were often antithetical to other cultures and societies and ideas, which threatened those, especially Islam, that hold to more traditional, autocratic, illiberal and theocratic concepts. America's popular culture—its music, films, food and style—clashed with these more constricted and traditional cultures. Against this tide of Americanism, people in many parts of the world began to identify more with ethnic and religions nationalism than with citizenship in artificially created nation states. The ability of the nation state to create homogeneous identifies for its people rapidly began to disintegrate.

A New Gilded Age

At home, relief from a half-century of confrontation with communism, coupled with a long economic boom throughout most of the 1990s, and worship of market values in the 1980s, produced a new American gilded age conspicuous for its materialism and consumption. A new generation of billionaires and a virtual new social class of mere millionaires led a social movement toward luxury home living in gated, privately secured communities, ever-expanding stock portfolios and high-style acquisitions.

The American media provided what relief they could from the stresses of vigilance by substituting entertainment for information, celebrity for facts, and gossip for ideas. The importance of the public interest gave way to the amusement of the exposé. The rise of the cult of celebrity and personality replaced serious public discourse. The ownership of media outlets moved from local, public-interested families to international, commercially interested conglomerates, more concerned with corporate profits than with informing the public about issues of consequence to national life.

Concurrently, American politics became more partisan, doctrinaire and orthodox, more media-dependent, more "attack"-oriented, more commercial, and therefore more costly. The cost of seeking and holding public office rocketed. Money from special interests moved in to fill the vacuum of demand, and dominated campaign financing. Lobbyists for powerful interests gained privileged access to public policy-makers from the president downward, and to "public" spaces as intimate as Abraham Lincoln's bedroom [in the White House]. The public, seeing the rights and interests of ordinary Americans being sacrificed to the exigencies of the politics of money and privilege, began to stay away from the polls. Cynicism replaced any sense of national cohesion.

In part because of the phenomena of the commercial republic and the age of acquisition, the age of ego, materialism and consumption—the so-called "bonfire of the vanities"—emerged. Private virtues, such as "family values", replaced public involvement and civic duty. A society of wealth and privilege, concerned for itself, came to dominate the social and political scenes.

The decade's "long boom" featured wealth flowing upwards: the creation of a new class of the rich, a middle class holding its own, and a widening gap between rich and poor. The rising economic tide did not lift the boats of the fourth quintile of the working poor or the fifth quintile of the structurally abandoned. The information revolution, globalisation, low-cost capital, low inflation, a housing boom and a reluctance to save all led to a gilded age of consumption not seen in America for almost a century. A nation increasingly divided along class lines was not a nation for whom cohesive national purpose was easily defined.

"Ask what you can do for yourself" became the motto of the 1990s. "Government is the problem", according to the new Reagan values. As a result, the best and brightest professionals and graduates shunned Washington and flocked to Wall Street and Silicon Valley.

Liberals and liberalism became increasingly more interested in broadening the net of individual and group rights, and abandoned any Sixties notions of public service or civic duty. Conservatives argued for the right to be left untaxed, unregulated and alone. The republic of the autonomous emerged. Few, if any, political leaders were heard in the last decade of the 20th century preaching national service, social obligation or the common good. The idea of serving the country, or of caring for the national interest, all but disappeared.

Thus, when the warnings came that a new danger was emerging in the form of terrorists employing weapons of mass destruction, few Americans at the dawn of a promising new century wanted to hear them. The 1990s were, in fact, a decade of forewarning, beginning with the first attack on the World Trade Center and ending with the second. In between, American interests and symbols were attacked around the world. The US leadership was continuously surprised.

The US Commission on National Security/21st Century, as noted above, warned that terrorism was coming. In its first public report in September 1999, entitled *New World Coming*, the commission concluded: "America will become increasingly vulnerable to hostile attack on our homeland, and our military superiority will not entirely protect us. Americans will likely die on American soil, possibly in large numbers." Very few listened. Preoccupied with what they perceived to be even more sensational stuff, the media mostly ignored these and other warnings, and consequently the public went largely uninformed.

When the attacks occurred, many Americans were heard to ask: "Why weren't we warned?" But the question is not coincidental; it is systemic. As an open society, is America doomed to experience a Pearl Harbor every few decades? Are Americans incapable of anticipation and preparedness? Or are we simply doomed to pursue our sleep?

America was caught off guard by post–cold war lassitude, a loss of national purpose, preoccupation with private acquisition, the revolution in warfare, the loss of confidence in government, major upheavals in global economics and polities and a failure to connect rights with duties.

But specific steps are available to guard against American slumber in the future. Public officials and institutions must be given responsibility and made accountable for early warnings and making sure the public is aware of impending dangers. Plans can be made for prevention of, protection from and response to attacks on the nation. Homeland security can and must be more than a passing fad. America does not have to slumber, nor does it always have to react. Now would not be too soon to consider measures—including the institutionalisation of entities such as the Commission on National Security, an effective intelligence review board and a highly trained, counter-terrorist National Guard—designed to prevent America from falling asleep again.

The CIA Contributed to the Attack on America

by Michel Chossudovsky

About the author: *Michel Chossudovsky is a professor of economics at the University of Ottowa, Canada, and director of the Centre for Research and Globalisation.*

A few hours after the terrorist events in New York City, Washington, D.C., and Pennsylvania, the Bush administration concluded without waiting for supporting evidence that "Osama bin Laden and his al-Qaida organization were prime suspects." George Tenet, director of the Central Intelligence Agency, stated that bin Laden has the capacity to plan "multiple attacks with little or no warning." Secretary of State Colin Powell called the attacks "an act of war," and President Bush confirmed in an evening televised address to the nation that he would "make no distinction between the terrorists who committed these acts and those who harbor them." Former CIA Director James Woolsey pointed his finger at "state sponsorship," implying the complicity of one or more foreign governments. And in the words of former National Security Adviser Lawrence Eagleburger, "I think we will show when we get attacked like this, we are terrible in our strength and in our retribution."

Meanwhile, parroting official statements, Western media commentators encouraged the launching of "punitive actions" directed against civilian targets in the Middle East. In the words of William Safire writing in the *New York Times:* "When we reasonably determine our attackers' bases and camps, we must pulverize them—minimizing but accepting the risk of collateral damage—and act overtly or covertly to destabilize terror's national hosts."

The following examines the history of Osama bin Laden and the links of the Islamic *jihad* (holy war) to the formulation of U.S. foreign policy during the Cold War and its aftermath.

Prime suspect in the September 11, 2001, hijackings, branded by the Federal Bureau of Investigation as an "international terrorist" for his role in the African

U.S. embassy bombings, Saudi-born Osama bin Laden was recruited during the Soviet-Afghan war "ironically under the auspices of the CIA, to fight Soviet invaders"—so reports the August 24, 1998, *London Daily Telegraph*. According to Fred Halliday in the March 25, 1996, *New Republic*, "The largest covert operation in the history of the CIA" was launched in 1979 in response to the Soviet invasion of Afghanistan in support of the pro-communist government of Babrak Kamal. And Ahmed Rashid writes in the November/December 1999 *Foreign Affairs:*

> With the active encouragement of the CIA and Pakistan's ISI [Inter Services Intelligence], who wanted to turn the Afghan jihad into a global war waged by all Muslim states against the Soviet Union, some 35,000 Muslim radicals from 40 Islamic countries joined Afghanistan's fight between 1982 and 1992. Tens of thousands more came to study in Pakistani madrasahs [Islamic fundamentalist schools]. Eventually more than 100,000 foreign Muslim radicals were directly influenced by the Afghan jihad.

The Islamic jihad was supported by the United States and Saudi Arabia, with a significant part of the funding generated from the Golden Crescent drug trade. Steve Coll writes in the July 19, 1992, *Washington Post:*

> In March 1985, President Reagan signed National Security Decision Directive 166 . . . [which] authorized stepped-up covert military aid to the mujahideen [Islamic freedom fighters] and it made clear that the secret Afghan war had a new goal: to defeat Soviet troops in Afghanistan through covert action and encourage a Soviet withdrawal. The new covert U.S. assistance began with a dramatic increase in arms supplies—a steady rise to 65,000 tons annually by 1987 . . . as well as a "ceaseless stream" of CIA and Pentagon specialists who traveled to the secret headquarters of Pakistan's ISI on the main road near Rawalpindi, Pakistan. There the CIA specialists met with Pakistani intelligence officers to help plan operations for the Afghan rebels.

The CIA's covert support was provided indirectly, using Pakistan's military ISI as a "go-between." Washington had concluded that, for these covert operations to be "successful," it must not reveal the ultimate objective of the jihad, which was to destroy the Soviet Union. The CIA played a key role in training the mujahideen by channeling CIA support through the ISI, which integrated the guerrilla training with the teachings of Islam. As Dilip Hiro of the International Press Service explains:

> Predominant themes were that Islam was a complete socio-political ideology, that holy Islam was being violated by the atheistic Soviet troops, and that the Islamic people of Afghanistan should reassert their independence by overthrowing the leftist Afghan regime propped up by Moscow.

Warriors Were Unaware of U.S. Assistance

The CIA's Milton Beardman stated, "We didn't train Arabs." Yet according to Abdel Monam Saidali, of the Al-aram Center for Strategic Studies in Cairo, bin

Laden and the "Afghan Arabs" had been imparted "with very sophisticated types of training that was allowed to them by the CIA." Beardman confirmed that Osama bin Laden wasn't aware of the role he was playing on behalf of Washington and reported bin Laden as saying, "Neither I, nor my brothers, saw evidence of American help."

Motivated by nationalism and religious fervor, the Islamic warriors were therefore unaware that they were fighting the Soviet army on behalf of Uncle Sam. And while there were contacts at the upper levels of the intelligence hierarchy, Islamic rebel leaders in theater had no contacts with Washington or the CIA. With CIA backing and the funneling of massive amounts of U.S. military aid, the ISI had developed into what Dipankar Banerjee described in the December 2, 1994, *India Abroad,* as a "parallel structure wielding enormous power over all aspects of government." The ISI had a staff composed of military and intelligence officers, bureaucrats, undercover agents, and informers, collectively estimated at 150,000.

> *"Saudi-born Osama bin Laden was recruited during the Soviet-Afghan war 'ironically under the auspices of the CIA, to fight Soviet invaders.'"*

Meanwhile, CIA operations had also reinforced the Pakistani military regime led by General Zia Ul Haq. According to Diego Cordovez and Selig Harrison, as quoted in an International Press Service review of their book, *Out of Afghanistan: The Inside Story of the Soviet Withdrawal:*

> "Relations between the CIA and the ISI had grown increasingly warm following Zia's ouster of Bhutto and the advent of a military regime." . . . During most of the Afghan war, Pakistan was more aggressively anti-Soviet than even the United States. Soon after the Soviet military invaded Afghanistan in 1980, Zia sent his ISI chief to destabilize the Soviet Central Asian states. The CIA only agreed to this plan in October 1984. . . . "The CIA was more cautious than the Pakistanis." Both Pakistan and the United States took the line of deception on Afghanistan with a public posture of negotiating a settlement while privately agreeing that military escalation was the best course.

Central Asia's Drug Trade

The history of the drug trade in Central Asia is intimately related to the CIA's covert operations. Prior to the Soviet-Afghan war, opium production in Afghanistan and Pakistan was directed to small regional markets. There was no local production of heroin. However, with CIA intervention, that changed. Alfred McCoy's study, "Drug Fallout: The CIA's Forty Year Complicity in the Narcotics Trade," in the August 1997 *Progressive,* confirms that, within two years of the onslaught of the CIA operations in Afghanistan,

> the Pakistan-Afghanistan borderlands became the world's top heroin producer, supplying 60 percent of U.S. demand. In Pakistan, the heroin-addict popula-

tion went from near zero in 1979 . . . to 1.2 million by 1985—a much steeper rise than in any other nation. . . .

CIA assets again controlled this heroin trade. As the Mujahideen guerrillas seized territory inside Afghanistan, they ordered peasants to plant opium as a revolutionary tax. Across the border in Pakistan, Afghan leaders and local syndicates under the protection of Pakistan Intelligence operated hundreds of heroin laboratories. During this decade of wide-open drug-dealing, the U.S. Drug Enforcement Agency in Islamabad failed to instigate major seizures or arrests. . . . U.S. officials had refused to investigate charges of heroin dealing by its Afghan allies "because U.S. narcotics policy in Afghanistan has been subordinated to the war against Soviet influence there." In 1995, the former CIA director of the Afghan operation, Charles Cogan, admitted the CIA had indeed sacrificed the drug war to fight the Cold War. "Our main mission was to do as much damage as possible to the Soviets. We didn't really have the resources or the time to devote to an investigation of the drug trade. . . . I don't think that we need to apologize for this. Every situation has its fallout. . . . There was fallout in terms of drugs, yes. But the main objective was accomplished. The Soviets left Afghanistan."

In the wake of the Cold War, the Central Asian region wasn't only strategic for its extensive oil reserves; it continued to produce three-quarters of the world's opium, representing multibillion-dollar revenues to business syndicates, financial institutions, intelligence agencies, and organized crime. The annual proceeds of the Golden Crescent drug trade—between $100 billion and $200 billion—represents approximately one-third of the worldwide annual turnover of narcotics, estimated by the United Nations to be of the order of $500 billion.

> *"Despite its anti-American ideology, Islamic fundamentalism was largely serving Washington's strategic interests in the former Soviet Union."*

With the disintegration of the Soviet Union, a new surge in opium production unfolded. According to UN estimates, the production of opium in Afghanistan in 1998 to 1999—coinciding with the buildup of armed insurgencies in the former Soviet republics—reached a record high of 4,600 metric tons. Powerful business syndicates in the former Soviet Union allied with organized crime to compete for strategic control over the heroin routes.

Serving America's Strategic Interests

The ISI's extensive intelligence military network wasn't dismantled after the Cold War, and the CIA continued to covertly support the Islamic jihad through Pakistan. New undercover initiatives were set in motion in Central Asia, the Caucasus, and the Balkans. Pakistan's military and intelligence apparatus essentially "served as a catalyst for the disintegration of the Soviet Union and the emergence of six new Muslim republics in Central Asia," reports the International Press Service.

Meanwhile, Islamic missionaries of the Wahhabi sect from Sáudi Arabia had established themselves in the Muslim republics, as well as within the Russian federation encroaching upon the institutions of the secular state. Despite its anti-American ideology, Islamic fundamentalism was largely serving Washington's strategic interests in the former Soviet Union.

Following the withdrawal of Soviet troops in 1989, the civil war in Afghanistan continued unabated. The

> *"Since the Cold War era, Washington has conciously supported Osama bin Laden, while at the same time placing him on the FBI's 'most wanted list.'"*

Taliban was being supported by the Pakistani Deobandis and its political party, the Jamiat-ul-Ulema-e-Islam (JUI). In 1993, the JUI entered the government coalition of Prime Minister Benazir Bhutto. Ties between the JUI, the army, and the ISI were established. In 1995, with the downfall of the Hezb-I-Islami Hektmatyar government in Kabul, the Taliban not only instated a hardline Islamic government but, according to Ahmed Rashid, also handed control of training camps in Afghanistan over to JUI factions. And the JUI, with the support of the Saudi Wahhabi movements, played a key role in recruiting volunteers to fight in the Balkans and the former Soviet Union. *Jane Defense Weekly* confirms in this regard that "half of Taliban manpower and equipment originates in Pakistan under the ISI."

In fact, it would appear that, following the Soviet withdrawal, both sides in the Afghan civil war continued to receive covert CIA support through Pakistan's ISI. In other words, backed by Pakistan's military intelligence, which in turn was controlled by the CIA, the Taliban Islamic State was largely serving U.S. geopolitical interests. The Golden Crescent drug trade was also being used to finance and equip the Bosnian Muslim Army (starting in the early 1990s) and the Kosovo Liberation Army (KLA). In recent months there is evidence that mujahideen mercenaries are fighting in the ranks of KLA-NLA terrorists in their assaults into Macedonia.

No doubt, this explains why, until recent events, Washington had mostly closed its eyes to the reign of terror imposed by the Taliban—including the blatant derogation of women's rights, the closing down of schools for girls, the dismissal of women employees from government offices, and the enforcement of the Sharia laws of punishment. . . .

A Cruel Irony

Since the Cold War era, Washington has consciously supported Osama bin Laden, while at the same time placing him on the FBI's "most wanted list" as the world's foremost terrorist. While the mujahideen are busy fighting the United

States' war in the Balkans and the former Soviet Union, the FBI—operating as a U.S.-based police force—is waging a domestic war against terrorism, operating in some respects independently of the CIA which has, since the Soviet-Afghan war, supported international terrorism through its covert operations.

In a cruel irony, while the Islamic jihad—featured by the Bush administration as "a threat to America"—is blamed for the terrorist assaults on the World Trade Center and the Pentagon, as well as the hijacking of the fourth plane downed in Pennsylvania, these same Islamic organizations constitute a key instrument of U.S. military-intelligence operations in the Balkans and the former Soviet Union.

In the wake of the terrorist attacks of September 11, the truth must prevail to prevent the Bush administration, together with its "coalition" partners, from expanding on a military adventure that threatens the future of humanity.

Lax Immigration Policies Contributed to the Attack on America

by Linda Bowles

About the author: *Linda Bowles is a nationally syndicated columnist.*

Our national borders are the front lines of America's war against terrorism. It should come as no surprise to anyone that our borders are being overrun. They are open doors to the easy entry, legal and illegal, of those who would do us harm.

The facts are beyond refutation. At this moment, there are more than 31 million people living in the United States who were born in a foreign country. This is an increase of 11.3 million, or 57 percent, since 1990.

An Increase in Illegal Immigration

At this moment, between 9 million and 10 million immigrants are illegally living in the United States. The illegal population in America has increased by an average of 500,000 per year for the last 10 years. None of them was checked for criminal records, diseases, ability to support themselves, or connections with terrorist groups.

Surely it must be clear, even to those who consider it an act of bigotry to restrict any kind of immigration, that if a poor Mexican laborer can successfully sneak into the country, so can terrorists whose primary purpose is to kill as many Americans as possible.

Some of those illegally in America came on student visas and never showed up for school. Others came on temporary visas of one sort or another, and stayed after their visas expired. We don't know where they are or what they are doing. There is no tracking system. There is no follow up.

In granting visas, we investigate backgrounds sloppily or not at all. We make no special effort to check out or bar entry to students or visitors from Iraq, Sudan, Iran, Libya, Syria, Cuba and North Korea, all of whom are on the State Department's list of countries that sponsor terrorist groups. They have no trouble entering our country.

Steven A. Camarota is director of research for the Center for Immigration Studies. In testimony prepared for the Senate Judiciary Committee, he said, "The current terrorist threat to the United States comes almost exclusively from individuals who arrive from abroad . . . America's borders are a major theater of operations . . . the weapons of our enemies are not

> *"If a poor Mexican laborer can successfully sneak into the country, so can terrorists whose primary purpose is to kill as many Americans as possible."*

aircraft carriers or even commercial airliners, but rather the terrorists themselves."

Dan Stein, executive director of the Federation for Immigration Reform, had this to say in a recent essay: "As we look around the United States, with the proliferation of ethnic communities where people remain culturally and ethnically separated from the American mainstream, it is apparent that the threads that hold this large and diverse country together are being threatened."

Two-thirds of the population growth in the United States since 1990 can be attributed to mass, unskilled immigration. For decades, immigration policies have been tilted toward Third World countries. Over 70 percent of the immigrants arriving in America during the 1990s came from Mexico, Central and South America, the Caribbean, and East Asia.

It is projected, to the delight of many, that by 2050, there will be no majority race in America. In effect, the government of the United States is redefining America through its immigration policies. It is doing so without once asking the American people what kind of a country they want America to be, in terms of culture, language, tradition, or even allegiance. In the minds of the ruling elite, diversity trumps unity as "our greatest strength."

Diversity Can Be a Weakness

Despite all the slogans, diversity can be a fatal weakness. Without unifying values and commitments, history informs us that ethnic diversity and multiculturalism often generate suspicion and hatred, fragmenting a country into hostile factions, tearing it apart at its ethnic and cultural seams.

The truth we need to face is this: America is suffering an immigration glut. Parts of America are like Third World countries. Hundreds of thousands of immigrants have no interest in learning the language or adopting the culture of their new country. They have formed separate communities that function as avant-garde outposts of their countries of origin. They offer a ready-made home base for terrorists.

For decades, liberal elitists and globalists have effectively squelched debate by labeling as "racist" or "uncaring" anyone who wished to talk honestly and realistically about the problem of immigration. For decades, the Democrat Party has nixed any attempt to stem the flow of Third World immigrants into America's slums and ghettos, knowing they would all vote the straight Democrat ticket. For decades, various businesses have welcomed and exploited cheap immigrant labor.

We need a totally new immigration policy, one which reflects the philosophy of Theodore Roosevelt: "There is no room in this country for hyphenated Americanism. . . . The one absolutely certain way of bringing this nation to ruin, of preventing all possibility of its continuing to be a nation at all, would be to permit it to become a tangle of squabbling nationalities."

Chapter 2

Is Anger Toward America Justified?

Hating America:
An Overview

by Mary H. Cooper

About the author: *Mary H. Cooper is a staff writer for the* CQ Researcher, *a weekly news and research report published by Congressional Quarterly, Inc.*

Shortly after the Sept. 11 terrorist attacks on New York and Washington, President George W. Bush posed a question that was undoubtedly on the minds of many stunned Americans. "Why do they hate us?" he asked the nation in an address before Congress.

"They hate what they see right here in this chamber—a democratically elected government," he continued. "They hate our freedoms: our freedom of religion, our freedom of speech, our freedom to vote and assemble and disagree with each other."

Anti-American Sentiment

Hatred of American democracy may help explain what drove 19 young Arab men to turn four commercial airplanes into weapons that killed themselves and nearly 5,000 innocent people. But many experts suggest deeper motivations as well—from resentment of U.S. policies in the Middle East to the perception that the American way of life is so offensive to Islam that it must be destroyed.

Still other observers say anti-American hatred has more to do with the haters than with America. "They hate us because they are a radical, utopian and totalitarian movement," says Daniel Pipes, director of the Middle East Forum, a Philadelphia think tank. "Like all such movements, be it fascism or Marxism-Leninism or this one, we are anathema in every detail and the main obstacle to the achievement of their goals. In a philosophical and a strategic sense, we are their enemy. So they have declared war on us."

But anti-American sentiment is not limited to Osama bin Laden and his Al Qaeda terrorist network, who have been linked to the attacks. The initiation of U.S. and British military action in Afghanistan prompted anti-U.S. street demonstrations in the Islamic world from the West Bank to Indonesia. Many demonstrators waved pictures of bin Laden and burned American flags. Mothers called on their sons to join the holy war against the United States. Clearly, the roots of such widespread anger extend beyond the delusions of a fringe group of zealots.

Grievances Against Infidels

Bin Laden himself has cited several reasons for his group's longstanding jihad, or holy war, against the United States. During a taped address broadcast on Oct. 7, 2001, by the Qatar-based television network Al-Jazeera, the multimillionaire terrorist listed numerous grievances against the American "infidels."

Topping bin Laden's list was the stationing of U.S. troops during the 1991 Persian Gulf War in his native Saudi Arabia, home to the Muslim holy cities of Mecca and Medina. He called Americans "those killers who have abused the blood, honor and sanctuaries of Muslims." As non-Muslims, Americans are viewed as infidels, and their presence in Saudi Arabia is considered an offense against Islam. Thus, the American soldiers stationed in Saudi Arabia are not seen as the defenders of one Islamic country—Kuwait—from invasion by another Islamic country—Iraq.

Bin Laden also condemned the United States for its support of international sanctions against Iraq, which were imposed in response to Iraqi leader Saddam Hussein's invasion of Kuwait and his refusal to allow U.N. inspections of suspected nuclear, biological and chemical weapons plants. Almost as an afterthought, bin Laden alluded in his Al-Jazeera address to U.S. support of Israel in the half-century-old Arab-Israeli conflict. He closed by vowing that "neither America nor the people who live in it will dream of security before we live it in Palestine."

Bin Laden's embrace of the Palestinian cause is widely considered more of a ploy to broaden his support among Muslims than a matter of great concern to him and his movement of disgruntled, mostly Saudi and Egyptian, nationals. "Bin Laden may not be very concerned about Israel, but a lot of people who support him are," says Daniel L. Byman, research director of the Center for Middle East Public Policy at the Rand Corporation, a Santa Monica, Calif., think tank. "More broadly, however, there is a general sense of resentment at the perceived humiliation of the Islamic world among certain segments of society. There's a perception that the Islamic community is not respected as it should be."

> *"Anti-American sentiment is not limited to Osama bin Laden and his Al Qaeda terrorist network."*

Globalization also plays a role in fanning anti-American sentiment by spreading U.S. economic and cultural influence throughout the world. "If you're poor, and the guy in the next village is poor, that's OK," Byman says. "But with globalization, people tend to compare themselves with bigger and bigger groups, and if you're in a poor village in Egypt what you see in U.S. television sitcoms are people with a lot of money."

Making matters worse, the televised image of the United States is often offensive in conservative societies. "When they think of America, they're not thinking of the land of Thomas Jefferson; they're thinking of the land of Britney Spears and jokes about sexuality on every sitcom they watch," Byman adds. "They're seeing a very disturbing social order that's quite different from what many of them envision for traditional society."

Demographic trends merely exacerbate the sense of powerlessness that feeds anti-American sentiment. As a result of rapid population growth and economic stagnation in recent decades, more than half the population of many Muslim and Arab countries today is under 25, and a good many are unemployed. In Egypt and Saudi Arabia, home to growing militant Islamic movements, universities are turning out more graduates than the local economies can absorb, adding to unemployment and resentment of repressive governments that receive support from the United States but do not use the money to relieve the economic suffering of their citizens.

> *"There is pervasive anger at the United States, but not pervasive hatred, which is held by only a few in the Middle East, such as Al Qaeda."*

Anger and Ambivalence

While the street demonstrations against the recent bombing of Afghanistan suggest that many of the world's 1.2 billion Muslims harbor anger toward the United States, many experts caution that these sentiments fall far short of the homicidal fury directed against this country by the likes of bin Laden.

"There is pervasive anger at the United States, but not pervasive hatred, which is held by only a few in the Middle East, such as Al Qaeda," says Shibley Telhami, a Middle East expert at the Brookings Institution. "That anger is driven by deeply held frustrations in the region with the existing political and economic order, which they see as oppressive to the majority. And they see America as the anchor of that order."

Counterbalancing that anger, in Telhami's view, is a genuine admiration for the United States and American life in the Muslim world—which includes 300 million Arabs. "Sure, there are a few who don't like America—the strong traditionalists who reject it on the basis of cultural values," he says. "But the vast majority of the people like a lot of things about America. They want American visas; they want American products. Like a spurned girlfriend, they want to win America."

But the carefully tempered statements of support for U.S. military action in Afghanistan by many Arab and Muslim governments suggest that public opinion toward the United States is ambivalent at best.

Anger About U.S. Policy in the Middle East Is Justified

by Larry Everest

About the author: *Larry Everest is a correspondent for the* Revolutionary Worker *newspaper and the author of* Behind the Poison Cloud: Union Carbide's Bhopal Massacre.

"Americans are asking, 'Why do they hate us'?" President George W. Bush stated in his nationally televised call to war. His answer was that "they hate our freedoms; our freedom of religion, our freedom of speech, our freedom to vote and assemble and disagree with each other."

I've covered the Middle East for more than 20 years—traveling to Iran, Palestine, and Iraq to investigate, first-hand, the impact that U.S. actions have had on the people in the region. I came away with a totally different understanding than this myth of "freedoms" told by George Bush.

Most people I met, and this included people from many different political trends, didn't hate "us"—they made a distinction between the U.S. government and people living in the U.S. But they did not view the United States as a place of "freedom." To them, the United States was an arrogant, cold-blooded, and hegemonic power—which has wreaked havoc with lives of the people in this region.

Beneath the earth, the vast oilfields of the Middle East and the Caspian Sea lie in an area of the planet that stretches from Algeria and Libya in the west to Afghanistan and Pakistan in the east, from Kazakhstan and Russia in the north to Saudi Arabia and Yemen in the south.

Before World War II, Britain and France had divided the region into "spheres of influence" and ruled them as colonies. But World War II severely weakened these old school colonialists, while the U.S. imperialists—who had deliberately maneuvered to come out on top of rivals and allies alike—emerged from the war ready to pick up the pieces of empire.

In the mid 1950s and early 1960s, U.S. imperial ambitions confronted a world where struggles for self-determination and national independence were sweeping the formerly colonized countries of Asia, Africa, and Latin America. A new rival—the once socialist Soviet Union—was mounting the stage and also seeking to expand into the Middle East.

The U.S. government dealt with these challenges ruthlessly: sometimes intervening directly, sometimes mounting covert operations to overthrow pro-Soviet or nationalist regimes, often arming and backing ruthless tyrannies.

One of the most notorious actions by the U.S. government in the Middle East took place in Iran in 1953, when the CIA organized the coup that overthrew the Mossadeq government after Mossadeq nationalized British holdings in the huge oilfields of Iran. With Mossadeq out of the way, the U.S. put the Shah, Mohammed Reza Pahlevi, on the throne, and backed his regime as a gendarme in the region and a military outpost on the Soviet Union's southern flank.

Under the rule of Reza Shah, the U.S. intensified its economic and political domination in Iran. For 25 years, this Shah ruled as an absolute monarch, torturing, killing, and imprisoning his opponents—especially radical and revolutionary-minded students.

Iran was not the only target of U.S. intrigue. In 1949 the CIA backed a military coup which overthrew the elected government of Syria. It aided the Egyptian government in hunting down pro-Soviet Egyptian communists, and in 1963 supplied Iraq's Ba'ath party (soon to be headed by Saddam Hussein) with names of communists, who the Iraqi regime then imprisoned or murdered.

Israel: America's Gendarme

Arming and supporting Israel—today to the tune of $3 billion a year—was another pillar of U.S. strategy in the region.

Created through violent dispossession of Palestinian people, the state of Israel was quickly recognized in 1948 by the United States—which had coldly refused to accept large numbers of Jewish refugees after World War II.

Today the Israelis are using live ammunition and U.S.-made attack helicopters against the Palestinian people's second "intifada." Based on land stolen from the Palestinians, the Israeli state became the U.S.'s gendarme in the region, ready to strike out against regimes that stood in the way of U.S. "strategic interests."

Israel's 1967 and 1973 wars not only expanded Israeli territory but were aimed at weakening surrounding Arab regimes, particularly Egypt—which was the heart of the Arab world under Nassar. The U.S. was eager to threaten and bribe Egypt to align with the U.S.—and not the Soviet Union.

> *"The United States [is] an arrogant, cold-blooded, and hegemonic power—which has wreaked havoc with lives of the people [in the Middle East]."*

In 1976 and again in 1982, Israel invaded Lebanon—killing more than 20,000

Lebanese and Palestinians, seizing southern Lebanon, and holding it until 2000. In 1983 the U.S., which had invaded Lebanon in 1958, once again sent troops—supposedly as part of a multi-national "peace-keeping" operation, but in reality to protect U.S. interests, including Israel's occupation forces. U.S. troops were withdrawn after a suicide bomber destroyed a U.S. Marine barracks.

The Invasion of Afghanistan

Jimmy Carter had declared Iran "an island of stability" in a sea of trouble. But in December 1978, more than 10 million people—a third of the population of Iran—took to the streets of Iran to demand an end to the rule of the Shah. The conservative Shi-ite Islamists led by Ayatollah Khomeini got the upper hand.

The Iranian revolution revealed to the world the deep and broad hatred of the U.S. and its allies in the Middle East. The 1980 seizure of the U.S. Embassy in Tehran—held for 444 days by Islamic students with the support of Iran's Khomeini regime—humiliated the United States and brought the end of Jimmy Carter's presidential career.

Then, in 1979, the Soviet Union invaded Afghanistan—which the U.S. rulers considered a "buffer state" between the Soviet Union to the north and the strategically important states of Iran and Pakistan to the south. The Soviets' immediate goal was propping up a friendly regime in Kabul, but the invasion significantly increased Soviet military presence in the region. For the U.S. ruler, the fertile crescent had become the "crescent of crisis."

> *"In 1988, the Iraqi regime launched mass poison-gas attacks on Kurds, killing thousands. . . . But during that time, the U.S. increased their support for the Iraqi regime."*

These were severe shocks to U.S. power in the region, and the U.S. responded by intensifying their rivalry with the Soviet Union—including by preparing for nuclear world war. This was Ronald Reagan's "resurgent America."

A key element of maintaining U.S. global power was maintaining its grip on the Persian Gulf and the world's oil supply—including keeping other Western imperialist rivals under the U.S. "nuclear umbrella." In 1979 U.S. President Jimmy Carter designated the Persian Gulf a vital U.S. interest and declared the U.S. would go to war to ensure the flow of oil.

At one point, when the U.S. feared a Soviet move into Iran during the turmoil following the revolution, Carter secretly put U.S. forces on nuclear alert and warned the Soviets they would be used if Soviet forces intervened in Iran. Zbigniew Brzezinski, national security adviser to Carter, called the elevation of the Persian Gulf to a "vital" U.S. interest a "strategic revolution in America's global position." Brzezinski told the U.S. security council: if we lose the Persian Gulf, we'll lose Europe.

Chapter 2

War and Intrigue in the Gulf

The U.S. attempted to deal with the new, more nationalist and anti-U.S. Islamic regime in Tehran with both carrots and sticks. It was even revealed that while U.S. personnel were being held in the U.S. Embassy in Tehran, representatives of soon-to-be President Ronald Reagan were negotiating with the Khomeini regime to delay the release of the U.S. "hostages" to better Reagan's chances in the 1980 election.

But the main U.S. gambit was to encourage Iraq to launch its 1980 invasion into southern Iran, which turned into a bloody eight-year war. Henry Kissinger summed up the cold-blooded attitude: "too bad they can't both lose." Over 1 million people were killed in the war, but it served U.S. purposes: it weakened both Iran and Iraq, and prevented them from causing the U.S. trouble elsewhere, especially in the nearby Gulf states.

The U.S. opposed UN action against the invasion, removed Iraq from its list of nations supporting terrorism, allowed U.S. arms to be transferred to Iraq, provided Iraq with intelligence aid, economic aid, and political support (the U.S. restored diplomatic relations in the late 1980s), encouraged its Gulf allies to lend Iraq over $30 billion for its war effort then, and looked the other way as Hussein gassed the Kurds at Halabja and other towns. All the better to weaken Iran's Islamic Republic, as well as draw Iraq away from the Soviet Union and closer to the U.S.

But for the U.S., Iran remained the bigger "strategic prize," so privately the Reagan government encouraged Israel to provide arms to Iran and then in 1985 secretly began shipping missiles to Iran itself. The missiles were supposedly a trade for U.S. hostages in Lebanon, but the bigger trade was for increased U.S. leverage in Iran. This secret plot collapsed when it was publicly revealed during the "Iran-Contra" scandal of the mid-1980s.

Covert War in Afghanistan

While the U.S. was trying to bully and intimidate Iran's new Islamic rulers, in next-door Afghanistan the U.S. was arming and organizing the Islamic fundamentalists—who had religious ties to the conservative Sunni Moslems of the Saudi Arabian ruling class. Within weeks of the Soviet invasion, the U.S. began a program of covert support to anti-Soviet Islamic Mujahideen fighters. In 1980, Osama bin Laden arrived in Afghanistan, bringing funds from the reactionary Saudi Arabian ruling class to the Mujahideen.

Over the next decade, the U.S. provided more than $3 billion in arms and aid to the Mujahideen—much of it financed through funding from Saudi Arabia and the rapidly growing heroin trade on the Pakistan-Afghanistan border. By 1987, 65,000 tons of U.S.-made weapons and ammunition a year were entering the war. Zbigniew Brzezinski wrote: "We now have the opportunity to give the Soviet Union its Vietnam."

The U.S.-Soviet rivalry produced a war that would tear Afghanistan apart.

More than one million Afghani people were killed and one-third of the population fled into refugee camps. Tens of thousands of Soviet soldiers died in the war. Twenty years later, the fighting in Afghanistan has still not ended.

The U.S. was lashing out at other states as well. In 1981 and again in 1986, the U.S. held military maneuvers off the coast of Libya in order to provoke a response from the Qaddafi regime. In 1981, when a Libyan plane fired a missile at U.S. planes penetrating Libyan airspace, two Libyan planes were shot down. In 1986, after a bomb killed two Americans in a Berlin nightclub, the U.S. charged that Qaddafi was behind it and conducted major air strikes against Libya, killing dozens of civilians, including Qaddafi's daughter.

In the Persian Gulf, the U.S. stepped up its direct military presence—organizing a "Rapid Deployment Force," increasing its naval presence, and pre-positioning equipment and supplies in the region. In 1987 the U.S. Navy was dispatched to the Persian Gulf to prevent Iran from cutting off Iraq's oil shipments. During these patrols, a U.S. ship shot down an Iranian civilian airliner, killing all 290 passengers.

> *"Since 1991, another 500,000 to 1,500,000 Iraqis have been killed by disease and malnutrition caused by U.S. sanctions."*

Today, the U.S. poses as the protector of the Kurdish people against Sadaam Hussein, but the history of U.S. treatment of the Kurdish—an oppressed nation of some 25 million living in Iran, Iraq, Turkey, and Syria—typifies the U.S. government's contempt for self-determination.

From 1973 to 1975, the U.S. supported Kurdish rebels in Iraq in order to strengthen Iran and weaken the then pro-Soviet Iraqi regime. But as soon as Iran and Iraq cut a deal, the U.S. withdrew support, denied the Kurds refuge in Iran, and stood by while the Iraqi government murdered them. Henry Kissinger, the U.S. National Security Adviser at the time, explained, "covert action should not be confused with missionary work."

Iran's Kurdish population rose up with millions of other Iranians to overthrow the hated Shah in 1979, but when they demanded their national rights, the U.S. government publicly supported the Khomeini regime's efforts to crush them and maintain Iranian domination of Kurdestan.

In 1988, the Iraqi regime launched mass poison-gas attacks on Kurds, killing thousands and bulldozing many villages. But during that time, the U.S. increased their support for the Iraqi regime.

Operation Desert Storm

The carnage and destruction of the Iran-Iraq war paved the way for the next war in the Persian Gulf—the U.S.-led Operation Desert Storm—Iraq was severely weakened after the eight-year war, and the Iraqi government felt its Arab neighbors owed them something—after all, they'd been fighting to protect

Saudi Arabia and Kuwait from the militant mullahs of the Islamic Republic of Iran, who were posing as the true defenders of Islam against Western influence and denouncing the pro-U.S. monarchies of the Gulf states. Instead, Iraq discovered that Kuwait was overproducing its oil quota, undercutting Iraqi oil revenues, and also slant drilling for oil into Iraqi territory. After warning the U.S. Ambassador that the situation was intolerable and that Iraq would take action—and after hearing from the U.S. Ambassador that this would pose no problem for U.S. interests—Iraq invaded Kuwait in August 1990.

The U.S. quickly condemned Iraq's invasion, fearing it threatened loyal clients in the Gulf and used the occasion to send a message to the planet.

On January 16, 1991, the U.S. launched Operation Desert Storm against Iraq and its people. For the next 42 days, the military might of the main imperialist power on the planet, joined by its allies, was unleashed on a poor Third World country. U.S. and allied planes pounded Iraq. By the time the war was over, they had dropped 88,000 tons of bombs. Then on February 22, 1991, the U.S. launched its 100-hour ground war. Heavily armed U.S. units drove deep into southern Iraq, leaving a trail of death and destruction in their wake.

During the war 100,000 to 200,000 Iraqis were killed. Since 1991, another 500,000 to 1,500,000 Iraqis have been killed by disease and malnutrition caused by U.S. sanctions.

New Rivalries, New Intrigues

The collapse of the Soviet Union and the dawning of a new millennium has only intensified U.S. designs to dominate the Middle East and Southwest Asia.

Two factors are key: the ever-growing dependence of the U.S. and its European and Japanese allies on foreign oil and the fact that most of the world's oil reserves are in this region.

The National Energy Policy Report estimates that U.S. oil consumption will rise 32 percent from 19.5 million barrels a day in 2000 to 25.8 million in 2020, yet domestic production will remain flat at 9 million barrels a day. This means that imports will have to rise 61 percent from 10 to 16.5 million barrels a day.

Where will this oil come from? The *San Francisco Chronicle* (9/26/01) reports that, according to the *Statistical Review of World Energy*, the Persian Gulf/Caspian Sea region accounts for more than 65 percent of world oil and natural gas production, and by 2050 it will account for more than 80 percent. The region's reserves are estimated to be 800 billion barrels of oil and an equal amount in natural gas. Meanwhile, energy reserves in the Americas and Europe are less than 160 billion and will be exhausted in the next 25 years.

A new element in this equation is the opening up of vast new oil reserves—estimated at 200 billion barrels of oil and 600 billion cubic meters of natural gas—in and around the Caspian Sea, bordered by Iran to the south, Russia to the north and west, and the newly independent republics of Kazakhstan and Turkmenistan to the east. This region used to be part of the Soviet Union, and the Soviet collapse has spawned new rivalries and intrigues over who will end up with control of these energy resources.

Some capitalists in the U.S. are maneuvering for a pipeline from Azerbaijan through Georgia to Turkey. Others dream of a pipeline from Turkmenistan across Afghanistan into Pakistan in order to link Central Asia directly to Western corporations and markets. The U.S. ruling class hoped Afghanistan's Taliban reactionary government could establish some stability in Afghanistan and allow these plans to proceed.

When the Soviet Union collapsed, many in the U.S. hoped for a cut in U.S. military spending and a "peace dividend." Today the U.S. military budget stands at $343.2 billion a year—23 times as much as the combined spending of the countries the U.S. calls its "likely adversaries" in the region.

Significant amounts of this spending are for forces aimed at the Middle East/Southwest Asian region, where the U.S. now has permanent military bases.

In October 1999, the U.S. Department of Defense shifted command of U.S. forces in Central Asia from the Pacific Command to the Central Command. Writing in *Foreign Affairs* ("The New Geography of Conflict," May/June 2001), Michael Klare notes, "The region, which stretches from the Ural Mountains to China's western border, has now become a major strategic prize, because of the vast reserves of oil and natural gas thought to lie under and around the Caspian Sea. Since the Central Command already controls the U.S. forces in the Persian Gulf region, its assumption of control over Central Asia means that this area will now receive close attention from the people whose primary task is to protect the flow of oil to the United States and its allies."

The government and media are billing America's New War as a conflict against "terrorism." But calculations of empire are, no doubt, the real agenda. George Bush warned the U.S. was preparing to "bring our enemies to justice or bring justice to our enemies." But justice is one thing the U.S. has never delivered in the Middle East. For the people of the Middle East, U.S. "justice" has meant shallow graves and shattered lives. This planet does not need another unjust war.

Anger About American Dominance Is Justified

by Doris Haddock

About the author: *Doris Haddock, also known as Granny D, is a retired secretary from Dublin, New Hampshire. She is the author of* Granny D: Walking Across America in My Ninetieth Year, *in which she details her cross-country walk in 1999 to bring attention to the need for campaign finance reform.*

It is hard to think clearly as we yet rock in the wake of the terrorist attacks on our cities and our people. But think clearly we must. Politics is a serious business. Not everyone cares to listen when people argue about the policies and practices of our political leaders. Americans would rather be painting their house or going to a good ball game than listening to a speech, and that is not a bad thing. We wouldn't get much done if we just argued politics all the time.

But there is a time for it, and this is that time. Our neighbors and children are being killed in great numbers because Americans are not in control of the American government, and haven't been for some time. And now we are being killed by our own airplanes, just as we were killed in our African embassies in 1998 by our own explosives, which we gave to the Islamic fundamentalists so that they would please kill our then enemies, the Russians.

And in May 2001 the current Bush administration gave $43 million to the Taliban Regime [the former government of Afghanistan] so that it would please kill our enemies, the heroin dealers of Afghanistan. Or was it to protect an oil pipeline? That's what we are now learning.

Our subcontracting of death has never done us much good, with Vietnam still the shining example, and with many other examples still bleeding in Central and South America, Africa, and in Southeast Asia.

The Coca-Cola company has been accused of financing the death squads in Columbia that kill union activists among the plantation workers. This so that our Coca-Cola is affordable to us. Wherever our large mining companies extract the value from foreign lands, we have a CIA and a military working to keep any leaders in power who will guarantee us a cheap labor supply and cheap mining products, at the expense of local people and their efforts toward democracy.

This is not who we want to be.

What America Wants to Be

If you ask the common American to describe the America he or she wants us to be, you will hear this: "We are the country that represents freedom, opportunity and fairness. We use our strength to help people around the world. We oppose brutal regimes and work toward world health and justice and democratic participation of all people. The Statue of Liberty is our beacon to the world."

The common American wants the American government to be that—to be that every day, in every corner of the world.

The common American would never answer: "America is this: We use our powerful military forces, intelligence forces, and our huge financial power to extract from weaker countries what we need for our own, affordable lifestyle in the US. We will support any brutal regime so long as they provide us with the cheap labor and materials we need, and so long as they keep any competing political systems out of the region. We will finance the massacre of peasants and workers, the torture of journalists and clerics, and the rape of nature and the sky itself so that we may live pleasantly today in America."

The common American feels ill at such words. And yet, that is the vision of America that many people in the world carry in their angry hearts. They see their miserable lives and their precious children and land being sacrificed for our luxury. They see our US-made helicopters and jets and guns and rockets suppressing and killing them. Naturally, they celebrate when we are made to suffer.

The disconnection between their perception and ours is profound: Our people are stunned at the idea that we are not universally loved.

Why America Is Hated

In classrooms all over America in the weeks following September 11, teachers and professors asked their students, "why do you suppose that some people around the world are so angry at us?" Many students no doubt suggested that differences in religion make some people intolerant and fanatically homicidal. What other reason could they have?

In a West Virginia college classroom last week, a friend of mine had something different to say.

"Look at it like this," he said to a classroom filled with honor students who couldn't imagine why America was under attack, except for reasons of religious extremism. "Imagine that West Virginia was a third world country," he said. "We have all this valuable coal, but there is one country, far away, that buys it all. They are the richest nation in the world, and they stay that way by getting our resources cheaply. They use their wealth to buy off our government officials, and to kill or torture any worker here who tries to organize a union or clean up the government. How mad would we be toward that distant country, and just how innocent would we think its citizens are, who drive around in luxury cars and live in elegant homes and buy the best medicines for their children, and otherwise live a life in sparkling skyscrapers—a life made affordable by the way they get resources from us? They admire their own democracy, turning a blind eye to what their government and their corporations do abroad."

The classroom was silent. "Well," he said, "that's pretty much what we do all over the world."

Someone at the back of the room said, "Well, we may not be perfect, but this attack didn't come from Central America or Africa or Southeast Asia, it came from wealthy people from the Mideast, for religious reasons."

> *"We will finance the massacre of peasants and workers, the torture of journalists and clerics, and the rape of nature . . . so that we may live pleasantly today in America."*

The class soon remembered that the US had supported the brutal regime of the Shah of Iran so to better protect the supply of oil to the US, and that the brutality of the Shah led to the rise of the Ayatollah Khomeini and the camp of violent Islamic fundamentalists, of which bin Laden was a product. The class was silent again. Then they began to discuss our problem, and they were in a position to come up with real answers.

Who Are Beating the War Drums?

So must all Americans see America as the world see us, so that we can strive for justice and the peace that comes with justice. The politics that killed six thousand people in New York September 11 [the number of dead was later revised to fewer than 3,000] is the politics of Mideast oil, the politics of the Shah of Iran and our support for him and his torture police—supported so that we might secure cheap oil and an anti-Communist puppet at any price to the local people and at any price to their democracy. The Shah did not deliver peace or safety, but instead he delivered into the world the Ayatollah Khomeini and the present wave of violent Islamic fundamentalists—who are no more Islamic in their practices than America's radical right are Christian in their practices. Both radical fringes are beating the war drums and accusing everyone who is not exactly like them of causing the September 11 horror. George Bush has declared war on evil. That is a holy war as chilling as the Taliban's call for war on evil.

This is not a time for all good Americans to forget their political differences and rally behind the man in the White House. The man in the White House should apologize for the most serious breach of internal security in the nation's history, not disguise his failure in calls for war. Can he hope that the fiery explosions in New York and Washington and Pennsylvania will be more accept-able to us if they are placed in a larger context of explosions of our own mak-ing? I do not rally around that idea. It is "wag the dog" taken to an extreme level, for he is not covering up his failure with a fake war, but with a real one.

He has taken every opportunity to make the world less safe, first in North Ko-rea and then in the Mideast and in Russia and in China. He needs a dangerous world to sell his military vision of the future. He is getting it. We must not go along with him.

The international community may soon have to rescue the Afghan people from the Taliban just as we had to rescue Europe from the Nazis, and rebuild it and let it find its way to self-government, but that is not the same issue and that will not resolve international terrorism at its roots. It is a diversion of our atten-tion from Bush's catastrophic failure at home and abroad.

Roosevelt's Four Freedoms

More than sixty years ago Franklin Delano Roosevelt delivered his "four free-doms" State of the Nation speech to Congress as he prepared the nation for war. In it, he laid down the sensible and humane preconditions for future world peace and democracy.

If Mr. Bush insists on preparing us for his war against evil, let him learn from that great speech.

Let me read you the final para-graphs:

"In the future days which we seek to make secure, we look forward to a world founded upon four essential human freedoms. The first is freedom of speech and expression—everywhere in the world."

"[Many people in the world] see their miserable lives and their precious children and land being sacrificed for our luxury."

Now Mr. Bush, do not tell us that we must prepare to lose our free speech rights and our rights to privacy, so that you and your corporate-military com-plex can continue to abuse the world safely. Do not take away our first freedom. You have installed your closest political associate as the head of FEMA, which has its own prison camps set up across America for any coming disturbances. We are indeed disturbed.

And now it seems we are to have an internal secret police, headed not by a law enforcement man but by Tom Ridge, and it is to be a cabinet-level position. This puts it far above the FBI, our non-political, professional internal security police, which has been discredited in an intensive campaign this year.

"The second," FDR continued, "is freedom of every person to worship God in his own way—everywhere in the world."

Do not, Mr. Bush, let your vision of good and evil and your friends on the re-ligious right overpower the religion of mainstream America, which is the reli-gion of peace and justice. Do not take away our second freedom.

"The third," said FDR, "is freedom from want, which, translated into world terms, means economic understandings which will secure to every nation a healthy peacetime life for its inhabitants—everywhere in the world."

We cannot live peacefully if we do not work every day for the people, not the despots, of the world—for justice, not for banking arrangements and trade agreements to fatten our already fat banks and corporations. Do not deprive the third world of this third freedom, for none of us are free if some of us are yet enslaved.

> *"None of us are free if some of us are yet enslaved."*

"The fourth is freedom," said FDR, "from fear, which, translated into world terms, means a world-wide reduction of armaments to such a point and in such a thorough fashion that no nation will be in a position to commit an act of physical aggression against any neighbor—anywhere in the world."

Let the US stop selling the weapons of death throughout the world. We have fallen far, far away from the vision of a peaceful, unarmed world. We are now the principle source of arms and high-tech weapons for all the despots of the world. Mr. Bush, you can only give us freedom from fear if the people of the world are free of fear. This the common American knows in his heart.

I remember Roosevelt's speech well. My husband and I no doubt discussed it at the dinner table. We had already been married 11 years at the time. I hope I speak for many common Americans who cannot see our flag without getting emotional with love for it. Our dream is that it should always represent the best that human beings can do on this earth. This is a time for us to rally around its best values and its highest dreams.

A Time to Speak the Truth

To the terrorists, here is my message: You are not martyrs, but cowards. Your selfish, ego-maniacal greed for a place in heaven cannot be purchased with the deaths of other people. Look across the Khyber Pass toward the land of Gandhi, who taught us that violence makes justice harder to come by, not easier. Today in America, the work of terrorists makes the work harder for those who want to reform America's policies and practices. You do not want to change American policies, or you would be using your millions to bring your message to us in ways that we can understand and act upon. You want only your shortcut to heaven. We have the same great God, the same Allah, and he shakes his head in sad disbelief at your spiritual immaturity.

"The ultimate weakness of violence," Dr. King taught us, "is that it is a descending spiral, begetting the very thing it seeks to destroy. Instead of diminishing evil, it multiplies it . . . Through violence you may murder the hater, but you do not murder hate. In fact, violence merely increases hate . . . adding deeper darkness to a night already devoid of stars. Darkness cannot drive out hate; only love can do that."

Terrorism makes it hard for us to do the right thing, but do it we must.

Old "Fighting Bob" LaFollette, that great reformer, said that "war is the money-changer's opportunity, and the social reformer's doom." But we will not accept doom. We will keep going. It is a time for all of us to speak the truth with courage and hope. America is, despite all, still the best hope for the world. But we are a work in progress, and we all have some work to do right now. It is the work of peace, of frank education, of making our lives and our communities more sustainable and less dependent on the suffering of others, and of cleaning up a campaign finance system that has allowed our elected leaders to represent not our interests and values, but those of international corporations who are set on world domination and who have the resources to buy our government away from us if we will let them. We will not, so long as we live, and so long as our four freedoms are our guiding lights and inspiration.

Anger About the U.S. Bombing of Afghanistan Is Justified

by Arundhati Roy

About the author: *Essayist and novelist Arundhati Roy is the author of* The God of Small Things, *for which she received the Booker Prize.*

As darkness deepened over Afghanistan on October 7, 2001, the U.S. government, backed by the International Coalition Against Terror (the new, amenable substitute for the United Nations), launched air strikes against Afghanistan. TV channels lingered on computer-animated images of cruise missiles, stealth bombers, tomahawks and bunker-busting missiles. All over the world, little boys watched goggle-eyed and stopped clamoring for new video games.

The U.N., reduced now to an ineffective acronym, wasn't even asked to mandate the air strikes. (As Madeleine Albright once said, "The U.S. acts multilaterally when it can, and unilaterally when it must.") The "evidence" against the terrorists was shared amongst friends in the coalition. After conferring, they announced that it didn't matter whether or not the "evidence" would stand up in a court of law.

Nothing can excuse or justify an act of terrorism, whether it is committed by religious fundamentalists, private militia, people's resistance movements—or whether it's dressed up as a war of retribution by a recognized government. The bombing of Afghanistan is not revenge for New York and Washington. It is yet another act of terror against the people of the world. Each innocent person that is killed must be *added to*, not set off against, the grisly toll of civilians who died in New York and Washington.

People rarely win wars, governments rarely lose them. People get killed. Governments molt and regroup, hydra-headed. They first use flags to shrink-wrap peoples' minds and smother real thought, and then as ceremonial shrouds to cover the mangled remains of the willing dead. On both sides, in Afghanistan as well as America, civilians are now hostage to the actions of their own governments. Unknowingly, ordinary people in both countries share a common bond—they have to live with the phenomenon of blind, unpredictable terror. Each batch of bombs that is dropped on Afghanistan is matched by a corresponding escalation of mass hysteria in America about anthrax, more hijackings and other terrorist acts.

There is no easy way out of the spiraling morass of terror and brutality that confronts the world today. It is time now for the human race to hold still, to delve into its wells of collective wisdom, both ancient and modern. What happened on September 11 changed the world forever. Freedom, progress, wealth, technology, war—these words have taken on new meaning. Governments have to acknowledge this transformation, and approach their new tasks with a modicum of honesty and humility. Unfortunately, up to now, there has been no sign of any introspection from the leaders of the International Coalition Against Terror. Or the Taliban [the former theocratic government of Afghanistan].

When he announced the air strikes, President George W. Bush said, "We're a peaceful nation." America's favorite ambassador, Tony Blair (who also holds the portfolio of British prime minister), echoed him: "We're a peaceful people."

So now we know. Pigs are horses. Girls are boys. War is Peace.

Infinite Injustice

Speaking at FBI headquarters a few days later, Bush said, "This is our calling. This is the calling of the United States of America. The most free nation in the world. A nation built on fundamental values that rejects hate, rejects violence, rejects murderers and rejects evil. And we will not tire."

Here is a partial list of the countries that America has been at war with—overtly and covertly—since World War II: China, Korea, Guatemala, Indonesia, Cuba, the Belgian Congo, Peru, Laos, Vietnam, Cambodia, Grenada, Libya, El Salvador, Nicaragua, Panama, Iraq, Sudan, Yugoslavia. And now Afghanistan.

Certainly it does not tire—this, the most free nation in the world. What freedoms does it uphold? *Within* its borders, the freedoms of speech, religion, thought; of artistic expression, food habits, sexual preferences (well, to some extent) and many other exemplary, wonderful things. *Outside* its borders, the freedom to dominate, humiliate and subjugate—usually in

> *"The bombing of Afghanistan is not revenge for New York and Washington. It is yet another act of terror against the people of the world."*

the service of America's real religion, the "free market." So when the U.S. government christens a war "Operation Infinite Justice," or "Operation Enduring Freedom," we in the Third World feel more than a tremor of fear. Because we know that Infinite Justice for some means Infinite Injustice for others. And Enduring Freedom for some means Enduring Subjugation for others.

The International Coalition Against Terror is largely a cabal of the richest countries in the world. Between them, they manufacture and sell almost all of the world's weapons, and they possess the largest stockpile of weapons of mass destruction—chemical, biological and nuclear. They have fought the most wars, account for most of the genocide, subjection, ethnic cleansing and human rights violations in modern history, and have sponsored, armed and financed untold numbers of dictators and despots. Between them, they have worshiped, almost deified, the cult of violence and war. For all its appalling sins, the Taliban just isn't in the same league.

The Taliban

The Taliban was compounded in the crumbling crucible of rubble, heroin and land mines in the backwash of the Cold War. Its oldest leaders are in their early forties. Many of them are disfigured and handicapped, missing an eye, an arm or a leg. They grew up in a society scarred and devastated by war. Between the Soviet Union and America, over 20 years, about $40 billion worth of arms and ammunition was poured into Afghanistan. The latest weaponry was the only shard of modernity to intrude upon a thoroughly medieval society.

Young boys—many of them orphans—who grew up in those times, had guns for toys, never knew the security and comfort of family life, never experienced the company of women. Now, as adults and rulers, they beat, stone, rape and brutalize women; they don't seem to know what else to do with them. Years of war have stripped them of gentleness, inured them to kindness and human compassion. They dance to the percussive rhythms of bombs raining down around them. Now they've turned their monstrosity on their own people.

> *"Afghanistan was reduced to rubble [in previous wars], and now, the rubble is being pounded into finer dust."*

More than a million Afghan people lost their lives in the 20 years of conflict that preceded this new war. Afghanistan was reduced to rubble, and now, the rubble is being pounded into finer dust. By the second day of the air strikes, U.S. pilots were returning to their bases without dropping their assigned payload of bombs. As one pilot put it, Afghanistan is "not a target-rich environment." At a press briefing at the Pentagon, Defense Secretary Donald Rumsfeld was asked if America had run out of targets. "For one thing, we're finding that some of the targets we hit need to be re-hit," he said. "Second, *we're* not running out of targets, Afghanistan is." This was greeted with gales of laughter in the Briefing Room.

On the ground in Afghanistan, the Northern Alliance—the Taliban's old enemy, and therefore the coalition's newest friend—is making headway in its push to capture Kabul. (Let it be noted that the Northern Alliance's track record is not very different from the Taliban's.) The visible, moderate, "acceptable" leader of the Alliance, Ahmed Shah Massoud, was killed in a suicide-bomb attack early in September 2001. The rest of the Northern Alliance is a brittle confederation of brutal warlords, ex-communists and unbending clerics. It is a disparate group divided along ethnic lines, some of whom have tasted power in Afghanistan in the past. . . .

The Alms Race

Reports have begun to trickle in about civilian casualties, about cities emptying out as Afghan civilians flock to borders that have been closed. Main arterial roads have been blown up or sealed off. Those who have experience working in Afghanistan say that by early November 2001, food convoys will not be able to reach the millions of Afghans (7.5 million according to the United Nations) who run the very real risk of starving to death during the course of this winter. They say that in the days that are left before winter sets in, there can *either* be a war, *or* an attempt to reach food to the hungry. Not both.

> **"Please,** *stop the war now. Enough people have died. The smart missiles are just not smart enough. They're blowing up whole warehouses of suppressed fury."*

As a gesture of humanitarian support, the U.S. government air-dropped 37,500 packets of emergency rations into Afghanistan. It says it plans to drop a total of 500,000 packets. That will still add up to only a single meal for half a million people out of the several million in dire need of food. Aid workers have condemned it as a cynical, dangerous, public-relations exercise. They say that air-dropping food packets is worse than futile. First, because the food will never get to those who really need it. More dangerously, those who run out to retrieve the packets risk being blown up by land mines. A tragic alms race.

Nevertheless, the food packets had a photo-op all to themselves. Their contents were listed in major newspapers. They were vegetarian, we are told, as per Muslim dietary law. Each yellow packet, decorated with the American flag, contained: rice, peanut butter, bean salad, strawberry jam, crackers, raisins, flat bread, an apple fruit bar, seasoning, matches, a spoon, a towelette, a napkin and illustrated user instructions.

After three years of unremitting drought, an air-dropped airline meal in Jalalabad! The level of cultural ineptitude, the failure to understand what months of relentless hunger and grinding poverty *really* mean, the U.S. government's attempt to use even this abject misery to boost its self-image, beggars description.

Put your ear to the ground in this part of the world, and you can hear the thrumming, the deadly drumbeat of burgeoning anger. Please. *Please*, stop the war now. Enough people have died. The smart missiles are just not smart enough. They're blowing up whole warehouses of suppressed fury.

Chapter 2

The Dangers of Hegemony

With all due respect to President Bush, the people of the world do *not* have to choose between the Taliban and the U.S. government. All the beauty of human civilization—our art, our music, our literature—lies beyond these two fundamentalist, ideological poles. There is as little chance that the people of the world can all become middle-class consumers as there is that they will all embrace any one particular religion. The issue is not about Good vs. Evil or Islam vs. Christianity as much as it is about *space*. About how to accommodate diversity, how to contain the impulse toward hegemony—economic, military, linguistic, religious, cultural and otherwise. Any ecologist will tell you how dangerous and fragile a monoculture is. A hegemonic world is like having a government without a healthy opposition. It becomes a kind of dictatorship. It's like putting a plastic bag over the world to prevent it from breathing. Eventually, it will be torn open.

It is important for governments and politicians to understand that manipulating these huge, raging human feelings for their own narrow purposes may yield instant results, but eventually and inexorably will have disastrous consequences. Igniting and exploiting religious sentiments for reasons of political expediency is the most dangerous legacy that governments or politicians can bequeath to *any* people—including their own. People who live in societies ravaged by religious or communal bigotry know that every religious text—from the Bible to the Bhagavad Gita—can be mined and misinterpreted to justify anything, from nuclear war to genocide to corporate globalization.

This is not to suggest that the terrorists who perpetrated the outrage on September 11 should not be hunted down and brought to book. They must be. But is war the best way to track them down? Will burning the haystack find you the needle? Or will it escalate the anger and make the world a living hell for all of us?

> *"Is war the best way to track [terrorists] down? Will burning the haystack find you the needle? Or will it escalate the anger and make the world a living hell for all of us?"*

At the end of the day, how many people can you spy on, how many bank accounts can you freeze, how many conversations can you eavesdrop on, how many e-mails can you intercept, how many letters can you open, how many phones can you tap? Even before September 11, the CIA had accumulated more information than is humanly possible to process. (Sometimes, too much data can actually hinder intelligence—small wonder the U.S. spy satellites completely missed the preparation that preceded India's nuclear tests in 1998.) The sheer scale of the surveillance will become a logistical, ethical and civil rights nightmare. And freedom—that precious, precious thing— will be the first casualty. It's already hurt and hemorrhaging dangerously.

Every day that the war goes on, raging emotions are being let loose into the world. The international press has little or no independent access to the war zone. In any case, mainstream media, particularly in the United States, have more or less rolled over, allowing themselves to be tickled on the stomach with handouts from military men and government officials. Afghan radio stations have been destroyed by the bombing. The Taliban has always been deeply suspicious of the press. In the propaganda war, there is no accurate estimate of how many people have been killed, or how much destruction has taken place. In the absence of reliable information, wild rumors spread.

Bush recently boasted: "When I take action, I'm not going to fire a $2 million missile at a $10 empty tent and hit a camel in the butt. It's going to be decisive." He should know that there are no targets in Afghanistan that will give his missiles their money's worth. Perhaps, if only to balance his books, he should develop some cheaper missiles to use on cheaper targets and cheaper lives in the poor countries of the world. But then, that may not make good business sense to the coalition's weapons manufacturers.

Guns and Oil

Then there's that other branch of traditional coalition business—oil. Turkmenistan, which borders the northwest of Afghanistan, holds the world's fifth largest gas reserves and billions of barrels of oil reserves. Enough, experts say, to meet American energy needs for the next 30 years (or a developing country's energy requirements for a couple of centuries). America has always viewed oil as a security consideration, and protected it by any means it deems necessary. Few of us doubt that the U.S. military presence in the Persian Gulf has little to do with its concern for human rights and almost entirely to do with its strategic interest in oil.

For some years now, Unocal has been negotiating with the Taliban for permission to construct an oil pipeline through Afghanistan to Pakistan and out to the Arabian Sea. From here, Unocal hopes to access the lucrative "emerging markets" in South and Southeast Asia. In November 1997, a delegation of Taliban mullahs traveled to America and even met with State Department officials in Washington and later with Unocal executives in Houston. At that time, the Taliban's taste for public executions and its treatment of Afghan women were not made out to be the crimes against humanity that they are now. Over the next six months, pressure from hundreds of outraged American feminist groups was brought to bear on the Clinton administration. Fortunately, they managed to scuttle the deal. But now comes the U.S. oil industry's big chance.

In America, the arms industry, the oil industry and the major media networks—indeed, U.S. foreign policy—are all controlled by the same business combines. It would be foolish to expect this talk of guns and oil and defense deals to get any real play in the media. In any case, to a distraught, confused people whose pride has just been wounded, whose loved ones have been tragically killed, whose anger is fresh and sharp, the inanities about the "Clash of

Civilizations" and the "Good vs. Evil" discourse home in unerringly. They are cynically doled out by government spokesmen like a daily dose of vitamins or anti-depressants. Regular medication ensures that mainland America continues to remain the enigma it has always been—a curiously insular people administered by a pathologically meddlesome, promiscuous government.

And what of the rest of us, the numb recipients of this onslaught of what we know to be preposterous propaganda? The daily consumers of the lies and brutality smeared in peanut butter and strawberry jam being air-dropped into our minds just like those yellow food packets. Shall we look away and eat because we're hungry, or shall we stare unblinking at the grim theater unfolding in Afghanistan until we retch collectively and say, in one voice, that we have had enough?

As the first year of the new millennium rushes to a close, one wonders—have we forfeited our right to dream? Will we ever be able to reimagine beauty without thinking of the World Trade Center and Afghanistan?

Hatred of America Is Not Justified

by Mona Charen

About the author: *Mona Charen is a nationally syndicated columnist.*

They cannot altogether contain themselves. The America-haters know that at a time like this, the vitriol they usually aim at the United States will not suit the national mood. And yet, it must truly gall them to remain quiet in the face of the most full-throated, unambivalent patriotism in 60 years.

This time, we did not choose a ribbon for our lapels to remember the victims. This time, we brought out our flag, the Stars and Stripes, because this time we need a symbol not just of sympathy, but of defiance.

And who could possibly fault the people of the United States—grief-stricken, furious, fearful—for this display of pride; this affirmation of our national spirit?

The America-Hating Left

Most of the America-despising left has fallen silent since September 11. But not all. Katha Pollitt, in the *Nation* magazine, writes: "My daughter, who goes to Stuyvesant High School only blocks from the World Trade Center, thinks we should fly an American flag out our window. Definitely not, I say: The flag stands for jingoism and vengeance and war. . . . It seems impossible to explain to a 13-year-old, for whom the war in Vietnam might as well be the War of Jenkins's Ear, the connection between waving the flag and bombing ordinary people half a world away back to the proverbial Stone Age. I tell her she can buy a flag with her own money and fly it out her bedroom window, because that's hers, but the living room is off limits."

Susan Sontag, the much-admired "American woman of letters," as the *New York Times* has characterized her, once swooned for Ho Chi Minh. Now, in the *New Yorker*, she condemns "the unanimity of the sanctimonious; reality-concealing rhetoric spouted by American officials and media commentators." Like Pollitt, Sontag will fly no flag from her living room. "'Our country is strong,' we are told again and again," she writes. "I for one don't find this entirely consoling."

It would be a mistake to think that these writers are cranks. The anti-American impulse of the left has been a constant feature of our national life for at least 70 years. While bald expressions of America hatred are comparatively rare in the present climate, other manifestations of this attitude have crept to the surface in the weeks following September 11.

We have heard a great deal, for example, about how the United States is only reaping what it has sown. Didn't we help to "create" Osama Bin Laden, it is asked, when we armed the Afghan resistance during the war against the Soviet Union? Well, yes, we did help the Afghans. And perhaps we erred in not foreseeing the radicalism this would engender among many Muslims.

> *"Our flaws are trifles compared with the ferocious evil that blights other parts of the globe."*

But has anyone mentioned the true culprit in causing Afghanistan's profound suffering? In all the reminders about our role in "creating" Osama Bin Laden, where is the condemnation of the Soviet Union for invading and wreaking havoc on that unfortunate country? If we are to be scolded for inadvertently creating a monster, what can you say of a nation that *advertently* invaded and plundered?

Denunciations of U.S. Policy

We have also been denounced for our policies against the Muslim world. As the *Weekly Standard* noted in a recent issue, left-wing Brits have been a bit less inhibited than their American cousins. England's *Guardian* newspaper, for example, accuses America of "constantly waging war against much of humanity: impoverished people mostly."

Is declining to stand by and see Israel obliterated our sin? Many on the left think it is. As for our recent actions regarding the Muslim world, columnist Charles Krauthammer neatly sums up: The United States has sent soldiers into harm's way three times in the past decade: Kuwait, Bosnia and Kosovo. In each case, we went to the aid of Muslims.

America hatred is much more a feature of left wing than right wing thought. Still, some Americans on the right (Jerry Falwell and Pat Robertson) could not resist the temptation to urge that this catastrophe was God's judgment on a sinful nation. That, too, amounts to sacrilege.

We have many faults. But one need look no further than the smoldering remains of lower Manhattan and the Pentagon to be reminded that our flaws are trifles compared with the ferocious evil that blights other parts of the globe.

Making Excuses for Terrorism Is Unacceptable

by Earl D. Rabd

About the author: *Earl D. Rabd is the founding director of the Perlmutter Institute for Jewish Advocacy at Brandeis University and a former executive director of the San Francisco area Jewish Community Relations Board.*

In the hours after the twin towers came crashing down on September 11, a tidal wave of support for a war against terrorism swept across the country; Americans had not been so united about anything in over a half-century. But almost immediately, an undertow of perverse opinion was created by the "semi-apologists"—those who deplore the acts of terrorism but, at the same time, shift an appreciable amount of the blame onto America. In so doing, they not only minimize the acts of terrorism, but suggest that those acts would stop if America would only behave more nobly.

Terrorism as a generic term can include the systematic use of terror against a military enemy. But the war we have declared is against the terrorism practiced and openly proclaimed by Osama bin Laden and his ilk, which primarily targets civilians. In 1998, one of bin Laden's organizations stated that the killing of American civilians was "the individual duty of every Muslim." It should go without saying that at least such murderous terrorism against innocent civilians breaks the bounds of civilized behavior and, on its face, can bear no excuse; unfortunately, it cannot go without saying. It is this kind of terrorism for which the semi-apologists do offer back-door excuses.

Their voices may seem no more than the usual chorus emanating from members of the anti-American and/or anti-Israel brigade, not likely to detract from the prevailing sense of outrage against these acts of serial homicide against civilians. But that outrage may not be enough. We may be facing a civilizational challenge much more difficult to understand than those of 20th-century fascism and bolshevism. Beyond aggressive military, diplomatic, and law enforcement action—and to sustain those action fronts long enough—this is destined to become an extended war for the minds of the American people. If their understanding of the real and portentous nature of this terrorism falters, the West, America, and Israel could suffer grievously.

The Refrain of the Semi-Apologists

The exculpatory note is found most clearly in the familiar refrain of the semi-apologists about the "root causes" of bin Laden's terrorism: the role of this country in visiting abject poverty on the Arab and Muslim world; and the arrogance and disrespect America generally shows towards that world, notably in its support of Israel. Noam Chomsky, Massachusetts Institute of Technology (M.I.T.) professor and pied piper to generations of college students, deplored the terrorist attacks, but then explained that they were committed out of feelings that "the US obstructs freedom and democracy, as well as material plenty for others. In the Middle East, for example, the United States supports Israeli oppression of Palestinians." Susan Sontag famously wrote in the *New Yorker* that while the slaughter in New York was inexcusable, it should really be seen as "an attack on the world's self-proclaimed superpower, undertaken as a consequence of specific American alliances and actions."

Rabbi Michael Lerner wrote in his magazine *Tikkun* that, while the terrorism was deplorable, it was partly explained by resentment about "the hoarding of the world's resources by the richest society in the world, and our frantic attempts to accelerate globalization with its attendant inequalities of wealth." The publications of the "Mobilization for Global Justice"—a sponsor of the often riotous "anti-globalism" protests against the World Bank and the International Monetary Fund—have been a venue for these semi-apologies.

And then there have been the universities. George Wright, a professor of political science at the University of California, voiced the refrain heard at many campus "peace vigils" when he said, "We should try to understand why there are people in the world that hate the United States." He explained that the terrorism in New York and Washington was an attack on America's economic dominance and leadership in "globalization." At the University of Texas, Professor Robert Jensen indicated that the mass murder in New York was "no more despicable than the massive acts of terrorism . . . that the United States has committed during my lifetime." A Rutgers professor told her students that the "ultimate cause [of the terrorism] is the fascism of US foreign policy over the past many decades."

> *"Murderous terrorism against innocent civilians . . . can bear no excuse. . . . [But] it is this kind of terrorism for which the semi-apologists do offer back-door excuses."*

Cynthia McKinney, Congresswoman from Atlanta, eminently qualified as a semi-apologist in a letter she sent to Prince Alwaleed bin Talai of Saudi Arabia. Mayor Rudolph Giuliani had rejected the ten million dollars given in aid of

New York's terrorist victims by the prince, who expressed his distaste for the slaughter while, at the same time, suggesting that the unfortunate American support for Israel had been a reason for it. In her letter to the prince, Congresswoman McKinney rebuked the mayor and moved swiftly beyond her description of the terrorist attack as "heinous," to state that "there are a growing number of people in the United States who recognize, like you, that the US policy in the Middle East needs serious examination." She approvingly quoted an Israeli peace group statement that "Israeli occupation of the West Bank and Gaza strip is the root cause of the violence and hatred."

Bin Laden's Root Causes

It is relatively easy, but not enough, to counter that causative logic by examining the expressed motivations of Osama bin Laden and the Qaeda terrorist network. Bin Laden has himself clearly explained his "root causes"; they do not notably include Muslim poverty, for which he offers no program, nor are they centered on the Palestinian cause. His primary purpose is to bring down the "quietist" Islamic regimes such as Saudi Arabia and Egypt. In an interview in an Arabic language magazine in November 1996, his main attack is on "the police states in the Arab world," starting with Saudi Arabia, from which he had been ejected. "In particular," he said, "the role of the religious organization in the country of the two sacred mosques is of the most ominous of roles." Those "weak and soft" clerics have corrupted Muslim youth with the connivance of the Saudi regime, which "placed the honest scholars in the jails."

> *"If the deprived Arab masses suddenly became prosperous, and if Israel turned over its nation to the Palestinians, [Osama] bin Laden's terrorism would not be abated."*

But the regime's most grievous sin was "to permit entry into the country of the two sacred mosques to the modern day crusaders," namely the Americans. The United States is seen as the main operational enemy because it supports the regimes of Saudi Arabia and other relatively "moderate" Arab states, helping to keep them out of the hands of bin Laden and his associates. It is also seen as enemy because it corrupts these countries and their youth with Western values of democracy and cultural permissiveness. Bin Laden founded the International Islamic Front for Jihad against Jews and Crusaders, which issued that fatwa imposing a religious responsibility on Muslims to kill Americans and their allies, both civil and military, "in any country where this is possible."

"Jews," not "Israelis," are named, along with "Crusaders" as targets in the full title of the International Islamic Front for Jihad. Bin Laden has said, "the enmity between us [the Muslims] and the Jews goes back far in time . . . and . . . war between us is inevitable." The Palestinian cause has crept onto bin Laden's agenda in the same formulaic way in which it has appeared on the far-Left agenda in

America, depicting Israel as the handmaiden of American imperialism in the Middle East. As an Egyptian columnist, Ab'd Al-Mun'im Murad, sympathetic to bin Laden's organization, Al Qaeda, put it: "The conflict that we call the Arab-Israeli conflict is, in truth, an Arab conflict with Western and particularly American colonialism. The US treats [the Arabs] as it treated the slaves inside the American continent. To this end [the US] is helped by the smaller enemy, and I mean Israel . . . the real issue is the Arab-American conflict."

A couple of weeks after the terrorist attacks on the US, Abdul Rahman Al-Rashid, in a Saudi newspaper, confessed confusion about reports that bin Laden was motivated by the Palestinian cause, writing that "never have I seen any reference [by bin Laden] to a political demand related to the occupied territories. . . . Of course, [there had been] general attacks on Zionism and the Jews [but] the Qaeda never made specific demands such as the establishment of a Palestinian state."

So, the "root cause" of bin Laden's terrorism is neither the poverty of the Arab and Muslim masses, nor the Israel/Palestinian conflict—nor America's role in either. If the deprived Arab masses suddenly became prosperous, and if Israel turned over its nation to the Palestinians, bin Laden's terrorism would not be abated.

A Political Conflict

But while bin Laden's motivation often needs to be countered on that level, it is too simplistic a level for any full understanding of the challenge of this particular terrorism. The problem—for America, the world, and Israel—goes beyond Al Qaeda, and well beyond the motivations of bin Laden and his personal agenda. This phenomenon is finally more political than religious in nature, and is the 21st century's first global challenge to the forces of democracy and freedom.

At least the barest outlines of Muslim history must now become part of the American consciousness. The "barest outlines" of a rich and complex history are always subject to point of view, but this much seems clear and relevant: Al Qaeda is a manifestation of the radical Islamism that is one wing of a severe conflict now coming to climax within the billion-strong Muslim world. Beginning in the 18th century, the Muslim world's recession from glory was propelled by the confrontation with a European West in its high tide of triumphalist technology and imperialism. Especially after some of the more rigorous restraints of colonialism were broken, many intellectuals and politicians of the Islamic world began to support policies of accommodation to Western modernism, some of which bore fruit.

In the gamut of opinion, however, there were always opponents who alternately proposed a thorough rejection of Western modernism and a return to the past. This was the soil out of which radical Islamism grew. This point of view was dramatically projected onto the world scene in the 1960s and 1970s, after a series of events perceived as setbacks, such as the defeat of Pakistan by India, the takeover by the Shah in Iran, the dissolution of the Syrian/Egyptian United Arab Republic—supposedly the base of the pan-Arab movement—and, yes, the defeat of Arab forces by Israel in 1967.

Radical Islamism, however, is driven specifically by a rejection of Western modernism. And whatever merit rejectionism might have in establishing "a new cultural entity," it has, by itself, proved to have little viability on the level of economics or statecraft. Islamist economic theories, for example, tend to be general and rhetorical, not much more than an extension of that rejectionism. One Islamist economist said, "[W]e will produce according to our capabilities and consume according to virtue."

> *"It is not true that America has had a serious historical role in creating [deprived conditions for the Muslim people]."*

This has essentially left radical Islamism as a utopian political movement without a program for dealing with the modern world or the deprived state of their peoples. In the words of Ray Takeyh, it has been reduced to "an ideology of wrath." Michael Ignatieff of Harvard has called it "an apocalyptic nihilism." Anger will not itself result in satisfying the real desires of the Muslim masses, but if they are offered nothing else, it could indeed provide the basis for a significant global political movement.

It is obviously true that an appeal of radical Islamism for many of the Muslim people lies in their economically and politically depressed state, especially when seen against the background of the former glory and considerable achievement of the Islamic civilization. It is also obviously true that, out of both humanitarianism and self-interest, America and the West should do whatever they can effectively do to help the accommodationist states overcome their deprived conditions. But it is not true that America has had a serious historical role in creating those conditions. Nor is it clear that the remedies lie in the utopian and vague nostrums of either the radical Islamists or some of the American semi-apologists. Whether "globalism" or controlled free market capitalism will hurt those deprived masses, or are their only solution, is a matter for serious debate, not sloganeering.

Moderate Regimes Have Precarious Control

Radical Islamism has not yet triumphed. It has been estimated that only 10 to 15 percent of the world's Muslims are supportive of the Ladenism that is an ultimate expression of the politics of anger. More than that, the accommodationist forces still control the bulk of the established Muslim states. But that control, in many of those states, is under siege. One Muslim scholar, Carl Brown, in his book, *Religion and State: The Muslim Approach to Politics,* has described the situation in these words: "The accomodationist/establishment forces were not only first in the field against the Western challenge. They have also been more important than the resistant/antiestablishment forces in terms of political power wielded. They continue to be so even today, although the cumulative weight of the Islamic radical forces may yet swing the balance to a degree unmatched during the past two centuries."

It is that "balance" that is at stake. Established regimes such as Tunisia, Algeria, Lebanon, Jordan, Morocco, and—notably—Egypt, plus even the Gulf states are engaged in a struggle with Ladenist terrorism, which has targeted many of them as "secular" regimes. One political analyst in Cairo, speaking anonymously to the Western media, said that "[i]f the Muslim Brotherhood [in Egypt] was legalized and allowed to run in genuinely free elections, it would almost certainly enjoy a runaway victory." The fact that such remarks are typically made "anonymously"—and that so many of the targeted Islamic regimes have offered such gingerly support to the coalition against terrorism—demonstrates the precarious control held by those regimes.

Some analysts of terrorism have suggested that such nihilistic movements are usually bound to fail in the end, but in this case, their initial success could at least result in the overthrow of a number of established Muslim states and their takeover by a triumphant radical Islam. Of course, a return to more traditional religious practices would presumably ensue, but that, including the ramifications for democratic practice, might be considered an internal Islamic matter. And some accommodationist tendencies could eventually redevelop, as they may be struggling to do in Iran. But for whatever time it endures, a radical Islamism in power would, predictably, only make matters worse for a large sector of the Muslim world and open up a more destructive and confrontational chapter for the whole world. For the sake of their unflagging support of the war against terrorism, Americans should understand these consequences, even if the moral outrage at any act of terrorism continues to burn.

Israel as a Background Factor

However, if there is a long-range battle for the American mind, the public will not be most vulnerable to the argument that America's "global" capitalism is either a credible cause of terrorism against this country, or one that should be readily abandoned. If frustration gathers, it is more likely that the public will be more vulnerable to attacks on American foreign policy in general, as exemplified by Pat Buchanan's populist attack on American "interventionism"; and that attack will center, as it does for Buchanan as well as for the Left, on America's support of Israel in particular.

To counter that line by the semi-apologists, it would not be credible to deny that the Palestinian/Israeli conflict is a background factor in this terrorism, even though it has only recently emerged on the agenda of bin Laden. The Arab world today represents only about a fifth of the Muslim world, and is not a dominant sector of Islamic politics. However, it is the cradle of Islam and a vehement center of radical Islamism. The control of non-Arab Afghanistan by the

Taliban owed much to the help of bin Laden and the incursion of Arab warriors from around the world. The result of the 1967 war in the Middle East, and the strong establishment of Israel in that area, shook the *Arab* world and obviously stimulated the rise of radical Islamism in that world. Israel, and its control of Jerusalem, became a symbol of the Western confrontation with Islam. This country's support of Israel ("the smaller enemy") is thus an exacerbating factor in the radical Islamist hostility to America. The cause of the Palestinian Arabs was not in itself high on the agenda of the Muslim world in general, nor even of the Arab states in the region. Indeed, the "Palestinian cause" did not seriously emerge until after the 1967 war. After that, however, it became a symbolic, highly exploitable item on the Arab and Islamist agenda—especially since there was a demonstrable contretemps about land, and a Palestinian displacement intensified by the fact that surrounding Arab countries placed so many of those Palestinians in "refugee camps," rather than absorb them.

> *"American resolve could be undermined by the specious semi-apologist suggestion that the Ladenists would refrain from terrorism if we would behave more nobly."*

In short, it cannot be denied that American support of Israel is a factor in Islamist hostility to the US. But it is also apparent that it is neither the prime nor the prior reason for Islamic hostility, or for terrorist activity towards this country—and neither would stop if America abandoned Israel. To the contrary, if America were to accede to terrorist demands that it pull away from Israel, it would only be seen as a terrorist success. Ensuing would not only be the immediate danger to Israel, but all the consequences of radical Islamism gaining leverage in its efforts to topple the regimes more open to future moderation.

American Sympathy Toward Israel

It may seem surprising that all the disinformation spread about the effect of America's support of Israel should have had so little initial effect on public opinion. Right after the terrorist acts in New York and Washington, surveyed American attitudes were found to have become even more favorable to Israel than before. Over the last quarter of a century, year after year, Americans have consistently said that they were more sympathetic to the Israelis than to the Arabs by a large margin. In the last 12 surveys with this language, more sympathy was expressed for the Israelis over the Palestinian Arabs by an average ratio of 45 to 13 percentage points. On September 14, that ratio was 55 to 7. Conventional wisdom once held that such favorability to Israel was tied to Israel's patent usefulness to America during the Cold War, and it was often suggested that such favorability might falter after the end of the Cold War. That did not happen. A strong factor in the American public's sympathy for Israel has always been the felt ties of common political and social culture. When asked, a large majority of Americans have said that Israelis are "more like us," as compared with Arabs. The positive interaction of Jews with other Americans during the past half-century has clearly played a role.

On the other hand, the measure of "sympathy" may be a weak reed on which to rest the predictability of the American public's support of Israel in a crunch; it does not take into account the question of how much Americans are willing to "sacrifice" for that sympathy. In the last four Gallup polls on the subject, between May of 1998 and July, 2000, 2 out of 10 Americans have consistently held that in the conflict between the Israelis and the Palestinians, the United States should take Israel's side, but 7 out of 10 have said that the United States "should not take either side." According to a *Newsweek* poll in October 2001, about 6 out of 10 said that America's relationship with Israel was a big reason for the terrorist attack, although at the time, the same proportion of Americans shrewdly agreed that if America moved away from Israel, it would not stop the terrorism.

The evidence is that American public opinion on support of Israel, while highly favorable, is not as deep as it might be, and in a crunch for America, both that opinion and the war against terrorism could be vulnerable to this theme expressed by the semi-apologists. This Israeli-connected theme is strengthened by certain tendencies of opinion expressed by many influentials who do not qualify as semi-apologists. One such tendency is exemplified by those media and public officials who—presumably in an attempt to be "fair" and "diplomatic"—overexercise the principle of equivalence. This often happens in company with a failure to acknowledge the legitimate role of self-defense in the arena of violence, as defined by the United Nations Charter. Thus, whenever there is an exchange between Palestinian terrorism and Israeli response, an abundance of media editorials will give them equal weight and call for equal subsidence. It is fair game for observers to criticize Israel when they think it overreacts or otherwise behaves unreasonably. But the automatic application of equivalence feeds the cause of those semi-apologists who are using Ladenist terrorism as a means of furthering their anti-Israeli or pro-Palestinian ideology.

A Struggle for the Minds of Americans

An exaggerated distinction between Palestinian and Ladenist terrorism serves the same purpose. Some Palestinian terrorists may have a more limited purpose than that of Al Qaeda, which is one of the reasons that bin Laden has not had it at the top of his agenda. On the other hand, Ha'aretz recently reported that of the first one hundred Palestinian suicide bombers in Israel, 66 belonged to Hamas, 34 to the Islamic Jihad. Both of these terrorist groups had core training in Al Qaeda camps, and are part of the radical Islamist network. There is no reason to believe that they would lay down their bombs or dismantle their anti-American hostility if this country were to withdraw its support of Israel. There is more reason to believe that if terrorist pressure were to cause America to withdraw its support—to the detriment of Israel, orthodox radical Islamism would even more thoroughly rule in the Palestinian state—to the detriment of Palestinian Arabs, and with little profit to America's image.

Perhaps the semi-apologists are most reprehensible in introducing any discussion at all of the "root causes" of a terrorism which is in itself inexcusable by any civilized and moral standards. They are largely impelled by the kind of philosophy simply expressed by the Russian anarchist, Mikhail Bakunin, that "everything that allows the triumph of the revolution is moral," voiced before him and after him by a number of nihilists, including those of radical Islamism. The tragic irony is that any serious effect the semi-apologists might have would directly contravene the "compassionate" goals in whose name they speak—whether for the condition of the depressed Islamic or Palestinian people, or the lessening of hostility and warfare in the world.

But whatever the consequences, the acts of serial terrorism will not stop until the Ladenist movement—beyond bin Laden himself—is destroyed. If this war is as extended and difficult as promised, at its core will be a struggle for the minds of Americans. Under burdensome circumstances, the resolve of the American people could be weakened if they don't understand the full import of this terrorism. And that American resolve could be undermined by the specious semi-apologist suggestion that the Ladenists would refrain from terrorism if we would behave more nobly, notably by withdrawing our support from Israel.

Criticism of America Is Often Oversimplified

by Todd Gitlin

About the author: *Todd Gitlin, author of several books on media and society, is a professor of journalism, culture, and sociology at New York University. As president of Students for a Democratic Society in 1963, he helped to organize the first national demonstration against the Vietnam War.*

As shock and solidarity overflowed on September 11, 2001, it seemed for a moment that political differences had melted in the inferno of Lower Manhattan. Plain human sympathy abounded amid a common sense of grief and emergency. Soon enough, however, old reflexes and tones cropped up here and there on the left, both abroad and at home—smugness, acrimony, even schadenfreude, accompanied by the notion that the attacks were, well, not a just dessert, exactly, but . . . damnable yet understandable payback . . . rooted in America's own crimes of commission and omission . . . reaping what empire had sown. After all, was not America essentially the oil-greedy, Islam-disrespecting oppressor of Iraq, Sudan, Palestine? Were not the ghosts of the Shah's Iran, of Vietnam, and of the Cold War Afghan jihad rattling their bones? Intermittently grandiose talk from Washington about a righteous "crusade" against "evil" helped inflame the rhetoric of critics who feared—legitimately—that a deepening war in Afghanistan would pile human catastrophe upon human catastrophe. And soon, without pausing to consider why the vast majority of Americans might feel bellicose as well as sorrowful, some on the left were dismissing the idea that the United States had any legitimate recourse to the use of force in self-defense—or indeed any legitimate claim to the status of victim.

America the Ugly?

I am not speaking of the ardent, and often expressed, hope that September 11's crimes against humanity might eventually elicit from America a greater respect for the whole of assaulted humanity. A reasoned, vigorous examination of

U.S. policies, including collusion in the Israeli occupation, sanctions against Iraq, and support of corrupt regimes in Saudi Arabia and Egypt, is badly needed. So is critical scrutiny of the administration's actions in Afghanistan and American unilateralism on many fronts. But in the wake of September 11 there erupted something more primal and reflexive than criticism: a kind of left-wing fundamentalism, a negative faith in America the ugly.

In this cartoon view of the world, there is nothing worse than American power—not the woman-enslaving Taliban, not an unrepentant Al Qaeda committed to killing civilians as they please—and America is nothing but a self-seeking bully. It does not face genuine dilemmas. It never has legitimate reason to do what it does. When its rulers' views command popularity, this can only be because the entire population has been brainwashed, or rendered moronic, or shares in its leaders' monstrous values.

Of the perils of American ignorance, of our fantasy life of pure and unappreciated goodness, much can be said. The failures of intelligence that made September 11 possible include not only security oversights, but a vast combination of stupefaction and arrogance—not least the all-or-nothing thinking that armed the Islamic jihad in Afghanistan in order to fight our own jihad against Soviet Communism—and a willful ignorance that not so long ago permitted half the citizens of a flabby, self-satisfied democracy to vote for a man [President George W. Bush] unembarrassed by his lack of acquaintanceship with the world.

But myopia in the name of the weak is no more defensible than myopia in the name of the strong. Like jingoists who consider any effort to understand terrorists immoral, on the grounds that to understand is to endorse, these hard-liners disdain complexity. They see no American motives except oil-soaked power lust, but look on the bright side of societies that cultivate fundamentalist ignorance. They point out that the actions of various mass murderers (the Khmer Rouge, bin Laden) must be "contextualized," yet refuse to consider any context or reason for the actions of Americans.

If we are to understand Islamic fundamentalism, must we not also trouble ourselves to understand America, this freedom-loving, brutal, tolerant, short-sighted, selfish, generous, trigger-happy, dumb, glorious, fat-headed powerhouse?

Not a bad place to start might be the patriotic fervor that arose after the attacks. What's offensive about affirming that you belong to a people, that your fate is bound up with theirs?

> *"In the wake of September 11 there erupted . . . a kind of left-wing fundamentalism, a negative faith in America the ugly."*

Should it be surprising that suffering close-up is felt more urgently, more deeply, than suffering at a distance? After disaster comes a desire to reassemble the shards of a broken community, withstand the loss, strike back at the enemy. The attack stirs, in other words, patriotism—love of one's people, pride in their endurance, and a desire to keep them from being hurt anymore. And then, too, the wound is inverted, transformed into a badge of honor. It is translated into protest ("We didn't deserve this") and indignation ("They can't do this to us"). Pride can fuel the quest for justice, the rage for punishment, or the pleasures of smugness. The dangers are obvious. But it should not be hard to understand that the American flag sprouted in the days after September 11, for many of us, as a badge of belonging, not a call to shed innocent blood.

> *"[In] reducing America . . . to a wicked stereotype, we encounter a soft anti-Americanism that . . . wheels automatically to blame America first."*

This sequence is not a peculiarity of American arrogance, ignorance, and power. It is simply and ordinarily human. It operates as clearly, as humanly, among nonviolent Palestinians attacked by West Bank and Gaza settlers and their Israeli soldier-protectors as among Israelis suicide-bombed at a nightclub or a pizza joint. No government anywhere has the right to neglect the safety of its own citizens—not least against an enemy that swears it will strike again. Yet some who instantly, and rightly, understand that Palestinians may burn to avenge their compatriots killed by American weapons assume that Americans have only interests (at least the elites do) and gullibilities (which are the best the masses are capable of).

Soft Anti-Americanism

In this purist insistence on reducing America and Americans to a wicked stereotype, we encounter a soft anti-Americanism that, whatever takes place in the world, wheels automatically to blame America first. This is not the hard anti-Americanism of bin Laden, the terrorist logic under which, because the United States maintains military bases in the land of the prophet, innocents must be slaughtered and their own temples crushed. Totalitarians like bin Laden treat issues as fodder for the apocalyptic imagination. They want power and call it God. Were Saddam Hussein or the Palestinians to win all their demands, bin Laden would move on, in his next video, to his next issue.

Soft anti-Americans, by contrast, sincerely want U.S. policies to change—though by their lights, such turnabouts are well-nigh unimaginable—but they commit the grave moral error of viewing the mass murderer (if not the mass murder) as nothing more than an outgrowth of U.S. policy. They not only note but gloat that the United States built up Islamic fundamentalism in Afghanistan as a counterfoil to the Russians. In this thinking, Al Qaeda is an effect, not a cause; a symptom, not a disease. The initiative, the power to cause, is always American.

But here moral reasoning runs off the rails. Who can hold a symptom accountable? To the left-wing fundamentalist, the only interesting or important brutality is at least indirectly the United States' doing. Thus, sanctions against

Iraq are denounced, but the cynical mass murderer Saddam Hussein, who permits his people to die, remains an afterthought. Were America to vanish, so, presumably, would the miseries of Iraq and Egypt.

In the United States, adherents of this kind of reflexive anti-Americanism are a minority (isolated, usually, on campuses and in coastal cities, in circles where reality checks are scarce), but they are vocal and quick to action. Observing flags flying everywhere, they feel embattled and draw on their embattlement for moral credit, thus roping themselves into tight little circles of the pure and the saved.

Avoiding Complexity

Faced with the uniquely murderous challenge of Al Qaeda, they see the old story of Vietnam, of Nicaragua, of Guatemalan peasants seeking higher pay in the coffee fields. The United States represents a frozen imperialism that values only unbridled power in the service of untrammeled capital. It is congenitally, genocidally, irremediably racist. Why complicate matters by facing up to America's self-contradictions, its on-again, off-again interest in extending rights, its clumsy egalitarianism coupled with ignorant arrogance? America is seen as all of a piece, and it is hated because it is hateful—period. One may quarrel with the means used to bring it low, but low is only what it deserves.

So even as the smoke was still rising from the ground of Lower Manhattan, condemnations of mass murder made way in some quarters for a retreat to the old formula and the declaration that the "real question" was America's victims—as if there were not room in the heart for more than one set of victims. And the seductions of closure were irresistible even to those dedicated, in other circumstances, to intellectual glasnost. Noam Chomsky bent facts to claim that Bill Clinton's misguided attack on a Sudanese pharmaceutical plant in 1998 was worse by far than the massacres of September 11. Edward Said, the exiled Palestinian author and critic, wrote of "a superpower almost constantly at war, or in some sort of conflict, all over the Islamic domains." As if the United States always picked the fight; as if U.S. support of the Oslo peace process, whatever its limitations, could be simply brushed aside; as if defending Muslims in Bosnia and Kosovo—however dreadful some of the consequences—were the equivalent of practicing gunboat diplomacy in Latin America or dropping megatons of bombs on Vietnam and Cambodia.

From the Indian novelist Arundhati Roy, who has admirably criticized her country's policies on nuclear weapons and development, came the queenly declaration that "American people ought to know that it is not them but their government's policies that are so hated." (One reason why Americans were not exactly clear about the difference is that the murderers of September 11 did not trouble themselves with such nice distinctions.) When Roy described bin Laden as "the American president's dark doppelganger" and claimed that "the twins are blurring into one another and gradually becoming interchangeable," she was in the grip of a prejudice invulnerable to moral distinctions.

Chapter 2

Insofar as we who criticize U.S. policy seriously want Americans to wake up to the world—to overcome what essayist Anne Taylor Fleming has called our serial innocence, ever renewed, ever absurd—we must speak to, not at, Americans, in recognition of our common perplexity and vulnerability. We must abstain from the fairy-tale pleasures of oversimplification. We must propose what is practical—the stakes are too great for the luxury of any fundamentalism. We must not content ourselves with seeing what Washington says and rejecting that. We must forgo the luxury of assuming that we are not obligated to imagine ourselves in the seats of power.

Generals, it's said, are always planning to fight the last war. But they're not alone in suffering from sentimentality, blindness, and mental laziness disguised as resolve. The one-eyed left helps no one when it mires itself in its own mirror-image myths. Breaking habits is desperately hard, but those who evade the difficulties in their purist positions and refuse to face all the mess and danger of reality only guarantee their bitter inconsequence.

Chapter 3

Are Measures Against Terrorism a Threat to Civil Liberties?

Civil Liberties and the War Against Terrorism: An Overview

by David Masci and Patrick Marshall

About the authors: *David Masci is a staff writer for the* CQ Researcher, *a weekly news and research report published by Congressional Quarterly, Inc. Patrick Marshall is a freelance writer and editor who writes about public policy and technology.*

As a Republican senator from Missouri, Attorney General John Ashcroft served on the Judiciary Committee. So when he testified on Capitol Hill on December 6, 2001, before his old panel, the camaraderie was palpable as he joked and reminisced with his former colleagues.

But the smiles quickly disappeared when the hearing—on civil liberties following the September 11 terrorist attacks on the World Trade Center and the Pentagon by Middle Eastern airplane hijackers—began in earnest. Democrats and Republicans alike closely questioned and even criticized Ashcroft on some of the tough, new policy changes made by the Bush administration in the name of national security—changes that critics say restrict cherished freedoms.

In particular, committee members worried that the Justice Department's continued detention of more than 600 mostly Muslim men may infringe on their rights. They also questioned Ashcroft's recent order permitting federal agents to eavesdrop on conversations between inmates and their attorneys. Until now, such communications have been considered privileged, or protected by law from disclosure. In addition, many senators worried that the president's plan to try foreigners charged with terrorist acts in secret military tribunals might lead to "victor's justice" at the expense of due process.

"The Constitution does not need protection when its guarantees are popular," said Committee Chairman Patrick Leahy, D-Vt. "But it very much needs our protection when events tempt us to, 'just this once,' abridge its guarantees of our freedom."

Ashcroft repeatedly dismissed panel members' concerns. "Our efforts have been crafted carefully to avoid infringing on constitutional rights, while saving American lives," he said.

In fact, the attorney general turned the tables and criticized his critics, arguing that they help the enemy when they oppose efforts to give the government more tools to fight terrorism. "To those who scare peace-loving people with phantoms of lost liberty, my message is this: Your tactics only aid terrorists—for they erode our national unity."

Restricting Liberties

The impulse to restrict liberties has always been and still is especially strong during wartime, and not just among the military and law enforcement communities. Polls show that the American people generally support the steps taken by the administration since September 11, just as they backed the last great raft of security measures—President Franklin D. Roosevelt's internment of Japanese-Americans and other restrictions enacted during World War II.

For instance, according to a recent *Washington Post*/ABC News survey, 73 percent of Americans favor allowing the federal government to eavesdrop on normally privileged conversations between suspected terrorists and their attorneys. The new rules . . . would be used in cases where the attorney general believed the person might be passing information to his lawyer that would further a terrorist act by their

> *"The impulse to restrict liberties has always been and still is especially strong during wartime."*

co-conspirators still at large. Ashcroft claims that discussions not involving terrorist plans will still be privileged and will not be used against the suspect.

But civil libertarians and others counter that lawyers and their clients need absolute privacy in order to speak freely when planning defense strategy. "An inmate won't feel like there is privacy, since the people who are prosecuting you are also the people who are listening into the conversation and deciding what is and isn't privileged," says Irwin Schwartz, executive director of the National Association of Criminal Defense Lawyers. Moreover, Schwartz says, there is an existing process—which involves acquiring a warrant from a judge—that allows officials to breach attorney-client privilege, but it at least requires the approval of a third, independent party.

A Fishing Expedition

Schwartz and others also have strongly criticized the Justice Department's initial arrest of more than 1,200 immigrants—mainly from predominantly Muslim countries—in the weeks following the attacks and the continuing detention of about half of them. Most are being held on immigration violations, but a small number are also being detained as possible material witnesses to terrorist acts.

Critics charge that in its efforts to prevent another attack, the department has essentially gone on a fishing expedition, rounding up Arabs and others without giving any real reasons that justify such a mass detention. "The federal' government needs to explain what it's doing here, needs to publicly show that these people are planning criminal activity or have engaged in criminal activity, instead of just throwing them in jail and not saying anything," says James Zogby, president of the Arab American Institute, an advocacy group for Americans of Arab descent. The secrecy surrounding the detentions is causing loyal Arab-Americans to feel threatened and disillusioned in their own country, he adds.

> *"73 percent of Americans favor allowing the federal government to eavesdrop on normally privileged conversations between suspected terrorists and their attorneys."*

Zogby and others are also disturbed by charges that some detainees have been held for weeks or even months with little or no evidence to link them to terrorist acts or groups. They point to Al Bader al-Hazmi, a San Antonio physician who was held for 13 days before being cleared, and Tarek Abdelhamid Albasti, an Arab-American and U.S. citizen from Evansville, Ind., who was detained for a week because he has a pilot's license. His detention came at the time authorities were investigating reports that Middle Eastern men were taking flying lessons in the United States, or seeking to rent crop-duster planes.

But Ashcroft has argued that his strategy of "aggressive detention of lawbreakers and material witnesses" has very possibly prevented new attacks. "This is an entirely appropriate reaction," agrees Kent Scheidegger, legal director at the conservative Criminal Justice Legal Foundation. "Given what happened on September 11 and the shadowy nature of the perpetrators, we need to look at a lot of people in order to effectively stop future acts of terrorism."

The Justice Department also says that none of the detainees have been denied their rights. "All persons being detained have the right to contact their lawyers and their families," Ashcroft told the Judiciary Committee.

Military Courts

At the same hearing, Ashcroft was called on, repeatedly, to explain and defend the administration's plan to possibly use military courts to try highranking, foreign terrorism suspects. The attorney general and other defenders of the proposal say that such courts may be needed because much of the evidence presented against defendants may be highly classified and not appropriate for use in an open court. In addition, they say, using traditional courts to try terrorists may endanger the lives of all of those involved, including the jury, prosecutors and judges.

But military courts, with their lower standards of due process, might not guarantee defendants a full and fair trial, says Ralph Neas, president of People for the American Way, a liberal civil liberties advocacy group. "This looks like a star chamber to me," he says. In particular, Neas worries that defendants may not be allowed to confront all of the evidence presented against them and that juries, made up of military officers, will be able to convict someone with a two-thirds vote rather than the usual unanimous verdict. . . .

The USA Patriot Act

Within hours of the September 11 attacks, lawmakers and commentators were calling for Congress to give new powers to the federal government to fight terrorism. And in spite of warnings by civil libertarians and some members of the House and Senate to tread carefully, Congress quickly complied, sending legislation to the president six weeks after the attacks.

Attorney General Ashcroft had asked for a variety of new powers in the weeks after the tragedy. In particular, Ashcroft requested new authority to conduct searches and detain suspects.

Exactly a month after the attacks, the Senate easily passed an anti-terrorism bill that had been crafted by Republican and Democratic leaders that encompassed many of Ashcroft's proposals. The following day, the House passed its own tougher version. Less than two weeks later, on October 25, the Senate cleared a compromise bill, 98-1. President Bush signed the USA Patriot Act the next day.

Although the bill was tempered somewhat by more liberal members of Congress, especially Senate Judiciary Committee Chairman Patrick Leahy, it gave Ashcroft much of what he had asked for, including provisions that:

• Allow "roving wiretaps" that follow suspects no matter what telephone they use. Old rules required law enforcement officers to acquire a new warrant each time a suspect used a different phone. The provision "sunsets" in 2005.

• Give law enforcement the authority to conduct "secret searches" of a suspect's residence, including computer files. Authorities can delay telling the suspect of the search for "a reasonable time" if such information would adversely affect the investigation. Previously, law enforcement had to inform suspects of any search.

> *"[Civil libertarians] object to those parts of the [anti-terrorism] law that allow the government to detain and deport or hold immigrants."*

• Allow the attorney general to detain any non-citizen believed to be a national security risk for up to seven days. After seven days the government must charge the suspect or begin deportation proceedings. If the suspect cannot be deported, the government can continue the detention so long as the attorney general certifies that the suspect is a national security risk every six months.

• Make it illegal for someone to harbor an individual they know or should have known had engaged in or was about to engage in a terrorist act.

• Give the Treasury Department new powers and banks and depositors new responsibilities in tracking the movement of money.

• Allow investigators to share secret grand jury information or information obtained through wiretaps with government officials if it is important for counterintelligence or foreign intelligence operations.

• Allow authorities to track Internet communications (e-mail) as they do telephone calls.

The Response of Civil Libertarians

While not entirely happy with the new law as written, many civil libertarians and others applauded Congress for not including all of the provisions requested by the attorney general. For instance, under Ashcroft's initial proposal, evidence obtained overseas in a manner that would be illegal in the United States would still have been admissible in an American court if no laws had been broken in the country where the evidence was gathered.

"So if you had a wiretap in Germany that would have been illegal here, but is legal there, the evidence would have been admissible here," Kent Law School's Professor Stephen Henderson says. "Congress said 'no way' and tossed that out."

And yet, Henderson and Georgetown University's Professor David Cole argue, even though it doesn't contain some of the most troubling provisions proposed by the Justice Department, the bill still goes too far. They particularly object to those parts of the law that allow the government to detain and deport or hold immigrants.

"I think the most radical provisions are those directed at immigrants," Cole says. "Under this law, we impose guilt by association on immigrants. We make them deportable not for their acts but for their associations, wholly innocent associations with any proscribed organization and you're deportable."

But George Washington University's Professor Orin Kerr argues that the Patriot Act does not, as critics contend, go too far. "Overall, I think this is a very balanced act, giving the government just what it needs in this fight," Kerr says. "I'm actually impressed at how narrowly tailored this language is. The administration could have gotten even more authority, but they asked just for what they needed."

"It's a gross overreaction to say that this new law is going to take away vital freedoms," agrees Catholic University's Professor Clifford Fishman. "It gives the government a bit more power than it had. And remember, this is a government that has generally shown that it can be trusted with power."

Anti-Terrorism Measures Threaten Civil Liberties

by Patricia Nell Warren

About the author: *Patricia Nell Warren, author of* The Front Runner *and* The Wild Man, *writes essays and commentary for various publications.*

Judging by what I see in the media, it's hard to know that America is at war. Other than bombing raids and anthrax scares at the top of the news, and flags fluttering on cars (already a bit tattered), and ongoing fundraising for U.S. victims of the terrorist attacks, it's business as usual. Advertising still shows us the glossy pre-9/11 world in which people's most picayune product choices get epic treatment. Looking at HGTV's dream homes and the Home Shopping Network's zirconium jewelry, we get little clue that thousands of people died in the World Trade Center, or that people are now dying in Afghanistan. The media do mull the country's economic woes, but this concern also preceded September 11. Paradoxically, it was the media's talking heads—as they watched the World Trade Center collapse—who told us that "nothing will ever be the same again." Since the major media are largely under the government's thumb, apparently the government wants us to believe that "nothing will be the same."

It's human to want life to go on as before. Even during World War II, which was the last time U.S. civilians felt personally threatened by a foreign attack, there were many efforts to re-establish normalcy—wartime romances, jukebox Saturday nights. Even in England and Europe, where civilians were directly savaged by the war, people cherished their nights without bombing raids and the rare little luxuries. What alarms me is not that desire for life to go on, but instead the collective denial that looms behind the search for normalcy—the denial that we're at war, the denial that our country is changing rapidly and drastically, giving up its commitment to democracy. There's a feeling that we want to get the war over fast, so we can get back to our pleasure-palace routine. Many Americans believe they can have their war and eat their cake too.

And yet, it's true that nothing will be the same again. Overnight we suddenly have prayer in schools, and few people are protesting because they're afraid of being called "unpatriotic." Overnight we have a degree of racial profiling and censorship and surveillance that wouldn't have been tolerated a year ago. Even so, this trend isn't really new. The United States had already been experiencing deep and radical change for some years. Our government, supported by many voters, now has well-established mechanisms for controlling people's behavior through an ever-expanding network of new laws covering everything from sex to smoking.

The Push to Criminalize Protest

In October 2001, by an overwhelming majority, Congress passed the anti-terrorist Patriot Bill, which has terrifying mandates for denying due process to suspects, while giving vast new powers to the president and law enforcement officials. Dissident voices in Congress are being silenced; most Congresspersons are afraid of being called "unpatriotic." But these new laws are only the tip of the iceberg. Just as dangerous, in my opinion, is the push to criminalize nonviolent civil disobedience and peaceful protest, a trend that has been gathering momentum for at least a decade. Nor is this trend a hidden one: it's right there in the open, in local headlines and courtrooms and police blotters. But not many Americans have paid real attention. Only a handful of civil libertarians have raised outcry at the vanishing of our liberties. Indeed, this ought to be a bipartisan issue, as the trend endangers the right to protest for both conservatives and liberals.

Traditionally in America, peaceful protest has been available when all else fails as a way of getting media and lawmakers to listen to grievances. Charges were usually in the misdemeanor category (meaning a year or less in county jail). Penalties were usually light—a few days behind bars, a small fine. But in the year 2000, as government and big business took alarm at the growing anti-globalization movement, a handful of Washington state demonstrators got slammed with the first felony convictions in American history. Now felony charges—"felony conspiracy to commit a misdemeanor trespass," etc.—are becoming commonplace. There are recent incidents where gay, lesbian, bisexual, and transgender protesters faced felony charges, notably in Illinois after the arrests during legislative hearings on the domestic-partners bill. Felony conviction is far more serious than misdemeanor, because it can put you in state prison for any-

> *"The anti-terrorist Patriot Bill . . . has terrifying mandates for denying due process to suspects, while giving vast new powers to the president and law enforcement officials."*

where from one year to life, and it drastically curtails your rights and privileges as a citizen for the rest of your life. In other words, a protester can have his or her life destroyed with a single felony conviction—and in many states a felon loses voting rights, too.

These stepped-up penalties for civil disobedience grew out of the get-tough-on-crime movement of the last two decades. As I study state criminal codes with their stiffened penalties for a wide range of charges like "criminal tres-pass," "criminal mischief," "resisting arrest," and "obstructing traffic," it becomes clear to me that lawmakers and law enforcement have know-ingly, quietly colluded on passage of crime-reform legislation that sends not only violent sex and drug offenders to prison for a long time, but also a wide range of nonviolent criminals, including nonviolent protesters. American government doesn't want to repeat the challenges to military and civil authority that happened in the 60's, when the country went up in flames over the Vietnam War and other issues. Perhaps the authorities knew that inevitably the pendulum of change would swing the U.S. back into a time of turmoil and questioning. Large demonstrations can leverage national opinion and national policy. Ameri-can authority evidently wants to eliminate that leverage.

> *"Since September 11, there has been a vast slackening of concern about civil liberties."*

Demonstrators or "Domestic Terrorists"?

At any rate, peaceful protesters—suffragettes who chained themselves to the White House gates, blacks who staged sit-ins at segregated lunch counters—are no longer viewed as guardians of American spirit. Legally they are viewed as "criminals" and will be prosecuted as such. The way the laws are now written, there is virtually nothing that the most peaceful mom-and-pop—or mom-and-mom—demonstrators do that won't get them dragged off in handcuffs. Indeed, some recent network news coverage characterized demonstrators as "domestic terrorists," lumping the peaceful protesters together with any who do commit violent crimes (assaulting police, starting fires, destroying property, etc.) during demonstrations.

This move to hamstring legitimate civil disobedience has gone unnoticed and unchallenged by most Americans. Indeed, since September 11, there has been a vast slackening of concern about civil liberties. Many Americans are so paralyzed by fear, that they will do anything, give up any freedom, to achieve "normalcy." As a friend of mine said, "With a recession on, and the need to make a living, American democracy goes to the bottom of the priority list for many of us."

I've already written several editorials in the gay press on vanishing civil liber-ties, and I'm concerned by the mild response they got—considering that gay people have everything to lose if civil disobedience becomes impossible. The original meaning of the word "gay activist" included a willingness to hit the streets and get arrested, if that's what it took. Indeed, some of our oldest gay ac-tivists came out of the anti-war movement. Back in the 60's, it was a badge of honor for an activist to have a long arrest record and spend a little time in jail. Now the anti-terrorist legislation creates a danger that racial profiling and persecution of minorities will be legitimized, which can include not only Arab-Americans but anybody whose activities or thinking are seen to jeopardize "national security." That certainly includes gay people.

Right now Mel White's SoulForce has been in the news as they tour the country, doing peaceful demonstrations at targeted church conferences, hoping to shame conservative Christians into greater tolerance of gay people. SoulForce's strategy is to communicate their peaceful intentions to police ahead of time, hoping to soften law enforcement's response. So far, they have been lucky to encounter misdemeanor charges for things like "blocking driveways," "disrupting a lawful meeting," etc. Inevitably, though, there may be the hard-nosed DA who slaps some SoulForce protesters with "felony conspiracy to block a driveway."

Today an activist's life can be destroyed by a single felony conviction. Under these circumstances, I wonder how many Americans will be willing to put their personal freedom on the line and walk the streets with a picket sign. I wonder how many gay Americans will be willing to risk their entire future to protest some bad decision on domestic partners, or sodomy laws, or gay adoptions, or gays in the military.

Americans Must Reclaim Liberties Now

While I oppose terrorism and believe that the USA must fight it, I also believe that Americans must act to reclaim civil liberties now. In a few years, when a body of hard-nosed court decisions and case law has shaped up, it will be harder to unstick these new laws. It falls to those of us who see the danger to act. In California, my editorials came to the attention of Senator Richard Polanco and his legislative deputy, Maria Armoudian. A working group of activists, trial lawyers, and media people, including myself, has helped draft a bill putting a cap on penalties for peaceful protest in California. Senator Polanco will be introducing it in the state legislature. As I write this, similar groups are forming in Colorado and Michigan. It is my hope that similar task forces will work to soften the laws in all fifty states. I hope that national civil liberties organizations will fully commit to this fight. We will also need to tackle federal law as well. It will be a long hard task.

Some commentators insist that the U.S. is already a police state. Whether this highly policed status quo becomes a permanent "American way" depends on whether enough Americans see the danger. We are even more in danger from our own anxieties about terrorism than we are from terrorism itself. That apocalyptic collapse of the twin towers that we all saw on TV mirrors an even more apocalyptic collapse that took place inside the minds of many Americans. Franklin D. Roosevelt's caveat, "The only thing we have to fear is fear itself," was never truer than today.

Military Tribunals Threaten Civil Liberties

by Jesse Jackson

About the author: *Jesse Jackson is founder of the National Rainbow Coalition, a social justice organization. He has been active in civil rights issues since the 1960s.*

We wage a war on terrorism to make America safe, to keep America free. President George W. Bush told the American people that although the terrorist attacks were designed to strike at our core freedoms as a democracy, they would not succeed.

One would think that the administration would be careful not to take away the very liberties that we set out to defend. But Attorney General John Ashcroft appears to march to a different drummer. He has goaded the White House into enacting by executive fiat the greatest encroachment of core American constitutional rights since the Supreme Court disgraced itself by declaring segregation the law of the land.

By executive order, the president has stripped some 20 million people in America of their right to a public and fair trial before a jury of their peers with an attorney of their choice. Anyone who is not a citizen—particularly the millions of hardworking legal residents who have come to this country to pursue their dreams and to seek citizenship—has by executive order been stripped of constitutional rights they once enjoyed.

Divorced from the Rule of Law

Mr. Ashcroft now claims the authority to investigate people without cause, to hold them without judicial review, to try them with secret evidence, before a secret military tribunal, where they have no choice of their own lawyer and no right of appeal. Evidence may be used that would be inadmissible in a civilian court, including documents whose origination cannot be validated. And the tribunal of military judges can convict them, without proof beyond a reasonable doubt, by a two-thirds vote. It can even sentence them to death.

The tribunals are so divorced from the rule of law that our Spanish allies are reluctant to extradite suspects to the United States for fear of violating core European human rights laws.

There is neither reason nor defense for these measures. Few would argue if the military tribunals were to try terrorists captured on the battlefield abroad. Even there it would be better to use international tribunals, as the one now in session to try Serbia's ex-boss Milosevic. But this order applies at home—even though the civilian courts are open here and fully able to dispense justice.

"Ashcroft now claims the authority to investigate people without cause, . . . to try them with secret evidence, . . . [with no choice] of their own lawyer."

The administration claims precedents from Abraham Lincoln's actions during the Civil War and Franklin D. Roosevelt's treatment of Nazi infiltrators in World War II. But the Supreme Court repudiated Lincoln's orders, which he admitted were outside the law. And Roosevelt's use of a military tribunal to try Nazi infiltrators was a limited, one-time-only treatment of spies for a nation with which we were at war.

The Ashcroft program allows for countless secret trials over the course of a conflict the president says will last many years and involve nameless opponents. And it's aimed not simply at terrorists but those suspected of helping them. The targets are not limited to al-Qaeda. Nelson Mandela, Yasser Arafat, the IRA, the Sandinistas, the Cubans and a range of other groups and leaders have been labeled as terrorists by the U.S. government over the years. As night follows day, you can count on dozens, if not thousands, of innocents being swept up in this maw.

An Untrustworthy Agenda

In response, the administration says, "trust us." But Ashcroft is not someone who inspires or merits trust. A man who sought to advance his political career by trashing that of a pre-eminent black jurist in a blatant misuse of his powers as senator is hardly the first person you'd think of entrusting with arbitrary power.

While the president has spoken out against hate crimes directed at Arab-Americans, the attorney general was announcing a program to investigate 5,000 Arab immigrants here on student or visitor visas—without any specific cause or suspicion.

And in the midst of the crisis, Ashcroft found time to pursue his own far right agenda—striking out to suppress the right of the elderly to choose a dignified exit under Oregon law, and the right of patients to get prescribed marijuana for medicinal purposes under California law. The attorney general allows neither states' rights nor individual rights to curb his expansive view of his own prerogatives.

And that is the point. The Founding Fathers included men like George Washington, who had earned immense trust. But they created a system of checks and balances based on the belief that trust was not enough. Power corrupts, they believed, and it must be checked and balanced to preserve the liberties that would make America . . . America.

In the *Washington Post*, eight former high-ranking FBI officials—including the most respected former director, William Webster—have raised serious concerns about Ashcroft's lock-'em-up campaign. Conservative Republicans like Rep. Bob Barr and liberal Democrats like Rep. Maxine Waters are expressing their alarm.

It is time for the Congress to call the attorney general to account, and to insure that the administration does not trample our liberties in the name of defending them.

Using Racial Profiling to Fight Terrorism Threatens Civil Liberties

by *Extra!*

About the author: Extra! *is a bimonthly journal published by Fairness and Accuracy in Reporting (FAIR), a media watchdog organization.*

Since September 11, 2001, there have been at least six bias-related murders and reports from around the country of assaults and harassment targeting Arab- and Muslim-Americans. Homes, businesses, mosques and Muslim schools have been vandalized, children tormented, and students harassed on college campuses.

Media have reported many of these assaults (e.g., *USA Today*, 9/20/01; *San Francisco Chronicle*, 10/4/01) and denounced them as what Tom Brokaw (*NBC Nightly News*, 9/20/01) called "one of the ugliest legacies of this crisis." "It's insanity to burden an entire people with the label terrorist," the *New York Times* pointed out (9/23/01), while a Long Island *Newsday* (9/18/01) op-ed counseled, "Don't Form a Lynch Mob to Fight Terrorism."

Mainstream media appeared unusually—and laudably—open to Muslim and Arab voices. Several outlets interviewed Arab- and Muslim-American advocates and clergy, giving them time to say, for example, that "Islam is a religion of peace" (*ABC News*, 9/25/01; *Baltimore Sun*, 9/17/01), and that Arab-Americans "love the flag" too (*Buffalo News*, 9/17/01). *CBS News* (9/13/01), straining to make a similar point, said that "Arab-Americans love their flag as much as we love ours."

As suggested by the reference to an Arab-American flag that is different from "ours," even as media called for sensitivity to anti-Muslim and anti-Arab discrimination, it was clear that sensitivity was not all journalists' strong suit. Reporting on the murder of Balbir Singh Sodhi, an Indian-American of the Sikh faith, the *New York Times* (9/19/01) noted that Sikhs, who wear turbans, "have attracted a disproportionate share of the anger following Tuesday's attacks." Readers might wonder just how much anger the *Times* would consider "proportionate."

Despite the article's headline—"Victims of Mistaken Identity, Sikhs Pay a Price for Turbans"—it's safe to assume the *Times* didn't mean to imply that Sodhi's murder would be any less senseless if he had actually been Muslim, as his alleged murderer (who described himself as "a patriot . . . a damn American all the way") presumably believed. So why not explicitly name racism or anti-Muslim bias, rather than "mistaken identity," as the cause of his death?

> *"The term 'Arab-looking' is virtually meaningless, encompassing not only Latinos and South Asians but also many whites and African-Americans."*

For some the attacks on the Arab and Muslim community were a non-issue. When ABC's Peter Jennings followed Bush's with-us-or-against-us speech to Congress with a Muslim imam's reaction (9/20/01), *Washington Post* TV writer Tom Shales called it a "bizarre choice journalistically" (9/21/01), questioning why the anchor would give "this much prominence and emphasis" to the issue of anti-Islamic bigotry. Days earlier (9/17/01), Shales called Jennings' broadcast "nauseating" because the host had the audacity to interview Palestinian parliament member Hanan Ashrawi about her views on U.S. foreign policy.

Beware the "Arab-Looking"

Quibbles about emphasis aside, most media denounced attacks on Arab- and Muslim-Americans. But there was nevertheless a strong current of support for a different sort of targeting: racial profiling.

Michael Kinsley argued in a *Washington Post* column (9/30/01) that racial profiling was "racial discrimination with a nonracist rationale": "An Arab-looking man heading toward a plane is statistically more likely to be a terrorist. . . . If trying to catch terrorists this way makes sense at all, then Willie-Sutton logic says you should pay more attention to people who look like Arabs than to people who don't. This is true even if you are free of all ethnic prejudices. It's not racism."

Given the broad range of features found in the Middle East, the term "Arab-looking" is virtually meaningless, encompassing not only Latinos and South Asians but also many whites and African-Americans. Like most post–September 11 advocates of profiling, Kinsley never explains how he knows that there is any correlation whatsoever between people who fit into this enormous category and any kind of security threat. One could as logically be wary of people from Milwaukee because Jeffrey Dahmer was a cannibal.

In "Survival Instincts Vs. Political Correctness" (*Washington Times*, 10/18/01), syndicated columnist Mona Charen made a sweeping demand for racial profiling: "Every Middle Eastern–looking truck driver should be pulled over and questioned wherever he may be in the United States." She also called for mass expulsions based on ethnicity: "There are thousands of Arabs in the United States at this moment on student and travel visas. They should all be asked, politely and without prejudice, to go home."

In "Profiles Encouraged"—subheaded, "Under the Circumstances, We Must Be Wary of Young Arab Men" (*Opinion Journal*, 10/19/01)—former Reagan speechwriter Peggy Noonan applauded acts of discrimination based on public anxiety: "I was relieved at the story of the plane passengers a few weeks ago who refused to board if some Mideastern-looking guys were allowed to board," she wrote.

Noonan also presented this as a positive story: "Two Mideastern-looking gentlemen, seated together on a plane, were eyeballed by a U.S. air marshal who was aboard. The air marshal told the men they were not going to sit together on this flight. They protested. The marshal said, move or you're not on this flight. They moved. Plane took off."

But perhaps law enforcement telling people where to sit based on ethnicity—a la Selma, circa 1955 [when black Americans were required to sit in the back of the bus]—shouldn't bother us: "If people are of Middle Eastern extract," Fred Barnes said on *Fox's Beltway Boys* (9/22/01), they "should be treated a little differently, just for the security of the United States." His colleague Mort Kondracke helpfully suggested that Arab-Americans themselves should "spread the word that this is not discrimination, you know, this is necessary."

> *"Ethnicity has never been a reliable indicator of who might be involved in terrorism, making racial profiling not only discriminatory but ultimately ineffective."*

Also on Fox (9/23/01), anchor Brit Hume said he wouldn't make a fuss "if I were an Arab-American and I had to spend a little extra time explaining myself to security guards getting on an airplane," since racial profiling is "reasonable" and "effective."

CNBC's Chris Matthews also saw the matter as simple enough. "When you know that all the trouble comes from one little part of the world, why don't you keep an eye on these people?" he asked (9/13/01). "This civil liberties answer is not going to work with a couple more of these disasters," he added. "I mean, 5,000 people are dead because we're big liberals, OK?" [The death toll was later revised to less than 3,000].

The Need to Be Smart

Leave it to Ann Coulter—whose racism was too much even for the Arab-bashing *National Review*—to reduce the pro-profiling argument to its fallacious core: "Not all Muslims may be terrorists," she allowed, "but all terrorists are Muslims" (*Yahoo! News*, 9/28/01).

That's just wrong, of course, as Timothy McVeigh, the Unabomber and decades of clinic-bombing, doctor-shooting Christian extremists can attest. The fact is that ethnicity has never been a reliable indicator of who might be involved in terrorism, making racial profiling not only discriminatory but ultimately ineffective.

One report that made this point was a *Today* show interview with law professor David Harris, who told Katie Couric (9/25/01): "Racial profiling doesn't work in general because when we get fixed on somebody's appearance, their racial appearance, their ethnic appearance, we miss important things about their behavior. And behavior is what good police work is all about."

Or as an unidentified pilot told NPR (*Morning Edition*, 9/25/01): "Our enemies come in all shapes, sizes, colors and descriptions, and as long as we just keep looking at people that look like that . . . they're not going to do that again. They'll do it a new way with a name like Smith or Jones. We want to be smart." That's a note that was too often missing from post–September 11 coverage.

Censorship of Unpopular Views Threatens Civil Liberties

by the National Coalition Against Censorship

About the author: *The National Coalition Against Censorship is an alliance of organizations that advocates the protection of the First Amendment.*

Here in New York, there were a few sources of comfort in the weeks after September 11, 2001: victims, firefighters, police and other rescue workers heroically risked, and some lost, their lives for others. Mayor Rudolph Giuliani (even though he's not so hot on the First Amendment) provided notable leadership to New Yorkers coping with unprecedented disaster.

As we dig out and try to restore normalcy, even though threats proliferate around the country, civil libertarians and others have begun to ask not only what harm terrorists may yet inflict, but also what damage will be self-inflicted in response to this threat. Individual liberties have historically been vulnerable in times of crisis. Already, national security concerns are cited to justify expanded government power to detain immigrants, monitor electronic communications, invade on-line privacy, control news coverage, and suppress dissent.

Dissent Has Become Unpatriotic

White House press secretary Ari Fleischer's warning to all Americans to "watch what they say," may have been deleted from the official transcript, but nonetheless spoke volumes. Overnight, dissent became unpatriotic and humor inappropriate. According to the *New York Times*, National Security Advisor Condoleezza Rice urged network executives to review statements by Osama bin Laden for "inflammatory language or potential hidden messages," even though his statements would be available from other news sources. Secretary of State Colin Powell reportedly asked the Emir of Qatar to exercise control over Al-Jazeera, a satellite channel, claiming that it is "inciting anti-Americanism" by showing U.S. bombardments and bin Laden statements. The Pentagon is keeping reporters away from military action, and selects the news that's fit to print.

Elsewhere in government the chill is apparent as well. California Representative Barbara Lee, who voted against congressional authorization for retaliatory military action, now needs security guards for protection, and Congressman Joe McDermott of Washington has come under fire for urging caution in responding militarily.

Professors, students, reporters and media figures have also come under attack for responding to the crisis in the American way: by questioning, analyzing, debating, and expressing opinions. TV talk-show host Bill Maher and writer-critic Susan Sontag were

> *"Government attempts to muzzle the press and control public opinion undermine the very rights we are fighting to preserve."*

excoriated for their views on what kind of conduct is "cowardly." *The Texas City Sun* dismissed a columnist for an article headlined "Bush has failed to lead U.S.," and a journalist was fired by the *Daily Courier* in Oregon for writing that it was an "embarrassment" that President Bush hid "in a Nebraska hole" while the Administration misinformed the public about threats to Air Force One. Professors in Florida and New Mexico have been placed on or taken leave, ostensibly for their own safety, after expressing unpopular political views.

Censorship of Art

The arts and entertainment have suffered as well. The cartoon, *The Boondocks*, by Aaron McGruder, was pulled from papers around the country for saying that the C.I.A. helped train Afghan rebels like bin Laden, and suggesting that the US has funded the Taliban. The Baltimore Museum of Art removed a piece of art because it contained the word "terrorist," and replaced it only after including an explanation of the artist's motivation. Even reading is suspect: one man was prevented from boarding a flight because the jacket cover of a book he was reading depicted dynamite!

Censorship in wartime to protect the safety and security of military troops and strategic information is understandable, but government attempts to muzzle the press and control public opinion undermine the very rights we are fighting to preserve. Liberties lost can become hard to restore.

The National Coalition Against Censorship has joined with the Society of Professional Journalists and others urging the Administration and Congress to respect First Amendment obligations to the public even in the fight on terrorism. Secrecy is permissible, according to the statement, only to the extent necessary "and only as long as necessary—to protect national security. . . . Journalistic scrutiny of the war on terrorism and publication of dissenting viewpoints are not signs of disloyalty to the nation, but rather expressions of confidence in democratic self-government and fulfillment of the First Amendment function of holding government accountable."

Expanded Police Powers Are Needed to Ensure U.S. Security

by Lamar Smith

About the author: *Lamar Smith is a Republican congressional representative from Texas. He is chair of the House Judiciary Subcommittee on Crime and serves on the House Science Committee and the Joint Economic Committee.*

Politics makes strange bedfellows, but so, too, do national tragedies. In the wake of the events of Sept. 11, 2001, we have seen new alignments in the ideological constellations. Congressional Democrats and Republicans literally have sung together and political-action groups whose differences once were deemed intractable now are laboring side by side. If the wolf and the lamb were to lie down together, it scarcely could be more surreal.

Why are Republicans and Democrats supporting the need for expanded police powers? Are they trying to give away, as some would suggest, our personal freedoms to the federal government? No, they are not.

The fact is that this area of law is not a zero-sum equation. The idea that restricting the freedoms of would-be terrorists entails a proportional reduction in one's own freedoms is what the president calls "fuzzy math." It simply is not the case.

The American Republic

When asked what kind of government the Founding Fathers had created, Benjamin Franklin replied to his inquisitor, "A republic, if you can keep it." It is a warning to all of us, the sons and daughters of America, that the forces of democratic government unleashed by us must also be tightly controlled by us. But there is more. "A republic, if you can keep it," implies not only an inward responsibility toward ourselves, against tendencies of bureaucracy and centralized authority, but also an outward one, against all those who would erase from the Earth our great experiment in human freedom. That is the struggle we face today.

Our republic is America, that shining city on a hill, and right outside the walls are the barbarian hordes who long to tear it down. But, like the Trojans of old, we already have brought our undoing upon us; not only are the enemies outside our walls, they are inside our gates.

That is why I support the Anti-Terrorism Act of 2001. [An amended version of the Anti-Terrorism Act—the USA Patriot Act—was passed in October 2001.] For the last several years, weakly enforced immigration policies have allowed the modern-day barbarians—suspected terrorists—to slip in and live in our midst. At the same time, the administration that loosened our immigration laws and their enforcement also oversaw a drastic reduction in the nation's intelligence apparatus. We were not asleep on our watch—we have not even been on watch for quite some time.

The Lessons of History

The United States has become so complacent with its position as the world's only superpower that we have forgotten the lessons of history. There once was another great republic called Rome. It, too, was the only superpower of its day. To ensure its own freedoms at home, Rome learned it had to promote certain freedoms and stability abroad. Just as Rome was not built in a day, neither was it quickly destroyed. The seeds of Rome's downfall were sown both without and within.

The "barbarian invasions" that we read about in history were not a mere series of well-orchestrated military campaigns by foreign groups. Rather they were more of a mass movement, an uprising of indigenous peoples. These peoples probably were not citizens but inhabitants, for the most part, who had filtered across the border and lived on the outer fringes of the empire for decades. Though they partook of the empire's bounty, the barbarians resented the wealth and power at its center, and for that reason they eventually sacked Rome.

The hubris of our hegemony lies in the fact that barbarians no longer travel in hordes but in hijacked airplanes full of innocent civilians. Such barbarity has thrust the United States into another war, one whose outcome will be determined not by the number of guns and bombs possessed but by the will and determination to use them. America now has the desire to bring to bear its weapons of war, but there are other resources in our inventory that we should not neglect.

Acting Accordingly During War

The intelligence community, no less than the conventional military, needs an infusion of fresh funds and energy. Furthermore, we cannot be afraid to let our intelligence networks gather critical information.

In the real world, the best intelligence often comes from the worst sorts of people. That is the very reason why they know what they do and are willing to sell out their friends for money. Congress recently has put onerous demands on the nation's intelligence-gathering apparatus by disallowing fraternization with certain unsavory types, but still expecting the same quality of information. The problem with this situation is illustrated by the old Texas saying, "When you wrestle with a hog you both get dirty, and the hog likes it." International terrorism is a dirty business. To come to grips with it, one sometimes must get dirty, too. The United States either has to learn to like it or be willing to pay for those who do.

> *"If some illegal immigrants or mob bosses were caught because of heightened border security and increased scrutiny, what's wrong with that?"*

Some still seem intent on continuing business as usual, in which case there soon may be no "business" or "usual" left. Americans have to realize that we are at war and act accordingly. A war requires that you do things differently than when you are at peace. Not only must our external-intelligence mechanisms change, but our internal ones as well.

The president has submitted his Anti-Terrorism Act of 2001 to Congress. . . . Although these may be desperate times we are living in, this is by no means a desperate measure. After reading the text of the proposed legislation, I have found it to contain none of the imagined threats against American's civil liberties. In all cases, the president asks for increased police powers against "suspected terrorists," not everyday American citizens. This legislation does not abrogate our time-tested requirements of search warrants and probable cause, nor does it seek to overturn our centuries-old common-law traditions. The only conceivable way this legislation can affect honest, hardworking Americans is by giving them increased protection against terrorism. The House soon will consider legislation designed to ensure that law enforcement has greater authority to investigate and pursue suspected terrorists. For those families searching for answers, and for those Americans who want security, this is necessary legislation.

Anti-Terrorism Measures

The Anti-Terrorism Act of 2001 is expected to address several key areas of law that deal with terrorism and that are badly in need of reform. The main areas of concern:

• Intelligence gathering. Expand law enforcement's ability to gain wiretaps and "trap-and-trace" authority, especially as it applies to electronic communications such as e-mails, as well as voice-mail messages.

• Criminal justice. Expedite court proceedings and increase penalties related to terrorism.

• Financial infrastructure. Expand the law to address laundering related to terrorist activity, provide for seizure of assets of terrorist organizations and provide trade-sanction authority.

• Immigration. Expand authority for mandatory detention of dangerous immigrants and better tracking of others, and promote interagency cooperation so that data is shared among agencies and used to its fullest extent.

In most instances, this legislation will apply only to noncitizens, who are not always entitled to the same constitutional rights as citizens. This bill provides us with the opportunity to redress years of lax enforcement of immigration policy and correct liberal excesses that have curtailed law-enforcement authority.

As a lawyer, I believe in our American system of jurisprudence, which teaches us that it is far better for some guilty persons to go free than for an innocent person to hang. But that theory has its limits. To say that our system sometimes requires that a few thousand innocents must die and the guilty party go free is an argument that I, for one, am not willing to make. And I suspect that 99 percent of the American people would agree with me.

Some civil-liberties advocates have termed the proposed measures "reactionary." To say that this legislation is a heat-of-the-moment, knee-jerk reaction to terrorism is hyperbole. If it were, the president would not even bother submitting the bill to Congress.

In fact, a bill I introduced Sept. 19, the Public Safety and Cybersecurity Act of 2001, was integrated into the Anti-Terrorism bill. The language for the bill was developed during the last several months and was completely unrelated to the terrorist events of Sept. 11. Unfortunately, those events tragically underscored the urgent need for such legislation.

Opponents of the legislation claim that its provisions could be used against ordinary citizens or a whole host of other groups, ranging from illegal immigrants to organized crime. Yet the language of the legislation makes it clear that it is directed solely toward "suspected terrorists." And even if some illegal immigrants or mob bosses were caught because of heightened border security and increased scrutiny, what's wrong with that? The majority should not pay for the hypersensitivities of the few, and the vast majority of Americans have nothing to fear.

Just because this legislation allows for heightened federal police powers to be used against suspected terrorists does not mean that such powers will be directed at you or me. Gen. George Patton once remarked that a soldier's duty was not to die for his country but to make enemy soldiers die for theirs. As citizens, we should never give up our freedoms but should make the enemies of freedom give up theirs. Unsubstantiated media reports warn that we as Americans are going to have to give up some of our liberties now. We do not have to, nor should we ever, and this legislation does not ask us to. Furthermore, we can be reassured that the courts will not be derelict in their constitutional duties and will continue to guard our liberties carefully.

The fundamental reason for government, the reason men always have banded together in community, is for the common defense. It is at times like these, the "times that try men's souls," that we must look to that defense and take the measures necessary to ensure it. The Anti-Terrorism Act of 2001 is a good first step in this direction, and that is why I support it.

Military Tribunals Need Not Erode Civil Liberties

by Joseph I. Lieberman

About the author: *Joseph I. Lieberman is a Democratic senator from Connecticut.*

President George W. Bush's Nov. 13, 2001, order authorizing military tribunals to detain and try foreign nationals accused of committing terrorist acts against the United States unleashed a firestorm of criticism, most of it suggesting that military trials grossly violate America's commitment to civil rights and civil liberties. That's truly unfortunate, because military tribunals have a long-settled and appropriate role to play in wartime, and the focus on whether to have military tribunals has obscured the far more important questions of what procedures those tribunals should follow and who should be subjected to them.

The Law of War

Although it may sound like an oxymoron to many, there is a body of international norms commonly referred to as the "law of war." It recognizes that armed conflict exists and inevitably involves death and destruction, but it also insists that combatants adhere to certain rules. Among them: warriors do not target civilian populations and they do not conceal their weapons or try to pass as noncombatants as they prepare for attack.

The attacks of Sept. 11 were acts of war. Because they were carried out against defenseless civilians by terrorists posing as noncombatants using concealed weapons, the perpetrators were guilty of heinous war crimes, not simple domestic crimes.

Throughout our history, both alone and in conjunction with other nations, we have used military tribunals to prosecute those accused of such crimes, and the Supreme Court has more than once upheld the executive branch's right to do so. The choice of military tribunals reflects a recognition that military venues are the appropriate place to understand, enforce and uphold our—and the international community's—decision to adopt rules to which all combatants must adhere.

The Practicality of Tribunals

Practical reasons also argue for accepting military tribunals. As others have pointed out, we can't expect those gathering evidence in a war zone to comply with all elements of the Supreme Court's Miranda decision [requiring law enforcement officers to inform suspects about their rights] or the Fourth Amendment's search-and-seizure rules. Nor is it apparent why triers of fact should be barred from hearing testimony about certain events sim-

> *"Military tribunals have a long-settled and appropriate role to play in wartime."*

ply because the testimony may not comply with the strict version of the hearsay rule found in the federal rules of evidence. And, given the threat al Qaeda poses to our civilian population, it is unclear why we would subject our judicial personnel and citizen jurors to the potentially lifelong consequences of involvement in a war crime trial when there is an accepted and legitimate alternative available.

Military tribunals must, of course, apply fair rules, consider only evidence that is truly trustworthy and accord defendants due process. But strict adherence to a process and a set of rules created for the prosecution of a completely different type of crime investigated under a completely different set of circumstances is neither necessary nor rational.

Military tribunals are a legitimate and accepted forum in which to accord alleged war criminals fair and impartial trials; they are not nor should they become an avenue in which to mete out second-class justice to any foreign national the government desires to detain. Yet no one can be blamed for reading the president's Nov. 13 order as allowing for just that.

The order did not clearly limit its application to those accused of war crimes, leaving open the possibility that the administration wrongly sought to extend military jurisdiction beyond its settled limits. The order left unstated whether a presumption of innocence would apply and what rights defendants would have to know the charges and evidence against them and to see their families or attorneys. Elemental aspects of due process such as the requirement that suspects not be held indefinitely without trial went unmentioned, as did any statement about whether proceedings would be open to the public.

Recent press reports indicate that the Defense Department is responding to these concerns and planning to issue regulations providing that fair procedures will govern in its military tribunals. Although it is impossible to reach a firm conclusion prior to the release of those regulations, the reports are encouraging.

The Need for Clarity

But the administration's misguided decision to charge Zacarias Moussaoui in federal district court rather than bring him before a military tribunal only makes it harder to convince the American people and the world of the fairness of our military tribunals. According to the government's indictment, Moussaoui willfully and knowingly conspired to kill and maim people in the United States, "resulting in the death of thousands of persons on September 11, 2001." In other words, the government believes Moussaoui took part in the preeminent war crime of the al Qaeda–Taliban engagement thus far, yet the government chose not to charge him in a tribunal established for precisely such actions.

When members of the Senate Armed Services Committee asked Defense Department officials for an explanation, those officials acknowledged that they hadn't even been consulted in the charging decision. According to a *Washington Times* article, Vice President Dick Cheney explained the decision as "primarily based on an assessment of the case against Moussaoui, and that it can be handled through the normal criminal justice system without compromising sources or methods of intelligence. . . . And there's a good, strong case against him."

With all due respect to the administration, these explanations cannot help giving ammunition to those who see the military forum as an arbitrary weapon rather than a fair tribunal. The decision to pursue a military trial should be based on the type of crime alleged—whether it is a war crime—and not the quality of the evidence against the accused. Regardless of whether the crime is a war crime, we should pursue individuals only when we have a "good, strong case" against them.

> *"Military tribunals are a legitimate and accepted forum in which to accord alleged war criminals fair and impartial trials."*

Military tribunals should not be used as leverage over those accused of war crimes or as a means to signal to those from whom we seek information or assistance that if they cross us they may disappear and receive second-class justice. Nor should such tribunals become a sign to either our own people or the world that the United States has abandoned its commitment to the rule of law and is willing to resort to more lax forums when it feels it can't make its case.

Properly constituted, military tribunals can provide now what they provided in the past: a fair, impartial means of trying and, if appropriate, punishing those who violate the laws of war.

Racial Profiling Could Be a Useful Tool Against Terrorism

by John Derbyshire

About the author: *John Derbyshire is a contributing editor of the* National Review, *a journal of conservative opinion.*

One thing that is fast becoming clear is that Americans at large are much more tolerant of racial profiling than they were before the terrorists struck. This fact was illustrated on September 20, when three men "of Middle Eastern appearance" were removed from a Northwest Airlines flight because other passengers refused to fly with them. A Northwest spokesman explained that under FAA rules, "the airline has no choice but to re-accommodate a passenger or passengers if their actions or presence make a majority of passengers uncomfortable and threaten to disrupt normal operations of flight."

Compare this incident with the experience of movie actor James Woods. Woods took a flight from Boston to Los Angeles one week before the World Trade Center attacks. The only other people in first class with him were four men "of Middle Eastern appearance" who acted very strangely. During the entire cross-country flight none of them had anything to eat or drink, nor did they read or sleep. They only sat upright in their seats, occasionally conversing with each other in low tones. Woods mentioned what he had noticed to a flight attendant, "who shrugged it off." Arriving in Los Angeles, Woods told airport authorities, but they "seemed unwilling to become involved." You can see the great change in our attitudes by imagining the consequences if the first incident had happened two weeks earlier, or the second two weeks later. The first would then have generated a nationwide storm of indignation about racial profiling, and stupendous lawsuits; the second, a huge police manhunt for the four men concerned. It seems very likely that Woods witnessed a dry run for the attack on the World Trade Center. One of the planes used in that attack was flying the same Boston–Los Angeles route that Woods flew. If the authorities had acted on his report—if, that is to say, they had been willing to entertain a little straightforward racial profiling—6,000 lives might have been saved. [The death toll from the September 11 attacks was later revised to fewer than 3,000.]

Civil libertarians are now warning us that in the current climate of crisis and national peril, our ancient liberties might be sacrificed to the general desire for greater security. They have a point. If truth is the first casualty in war, liberty is often the second. The reason that practically nobody can afford to live in Manhattan who isn't already living there is rent control, a World War II measure, never repealed, that removed a landlord's freedom to let his property at whatever rent the market would bear. But the moral to be drawn from that instance is only that, as legal scholar Bruce Ackerman has recently argued, emergency legislation must never be enacted without a clear "sunset provision": after some fixed period—Ackerman suggests two years—the law must lapse. The civil-liberties crowd does not, in any case, have a dazzling record on the liberties involved in private commercial transactions. What happened to a cabdriver's liberty to use his own judgment about which passengers to pick up? Gone, swept away in the racial-profiling panic of the 1990s, along with the lives of several cabbies.

The Potential for Confusion

It is in the matter of proactive law enforcement—the kinds of things that police agencies do to prevent crime or terrorism—that our liberties are most at risk in tense times. Whom should you wiretap? Whom should airport security take in for questioning? This is where racial profiling kicks in, with all its ambiguities. Just take a careful look, for example, at that phrase, "of Middle Eastern appearance," which I imagine security agencies are already abbreviating OMEA. The last time I wrote about this subject, I concentrated on the topics that were in the air at that time: the disproportionate attention police officers give to black and Hispanic persons as crime suspects, and the targeting of Wen Ho Lee in the nuclear-espionage case. I had nothing to say about terrorists from the Middle East, or people who might be thought to look like them. OMEA was not, at that point, an issue.

Now it is, and the problem is that OMEA is perhaps a more dubious description even than "black" or "Hispanic." You can see the difficulties by scanning the photographs of the September 11 hijackers published in our newspapers. A few are unmistakably OMEA. My reaction on seeing the photograph of the first to be identified, Mohamed Atta, was that he looked exactly like my own mental conception of an Arab terrorist. On the other hand, one of his companions on AA Flight 11, Wail al-Shehri, is the spitting image of a boy I went to school with—a boy of

> *"Profiling is an aid—very far from an infallible one, but still a useful one—to identifying those who want to harm us."*

entirely English origins, whose name was Hobson. Ahmed al-Nami (UA Flight 93) looks like a Welsh punk rocker. And so on.

Other visual markers offer similar opportunities for confusion. This fellow with a beard and a turban, coming down the road—he must surely be an Arab, or at least a Muslim? Well, maybe, but he is much more likely to be a Sikh—belonging, that is, to a religion that owes more to Hinduism than to Islam, practiced by non-Arab peoples who speak Indo-European languages, and with scriptures written with a Hindi-style script, not an Arabic one. Sikhism requires male adherents to keep an untrimmed beard and wear a turban; Islam does not.

> *"So long as the authorities treat everyone with courtesy and apologize to the inconvenienced innocent, racial profiling is a ... sensible tool."*

Most other attempts at a "Middle Eastern" typology fail a lot of the time, too. Middle Easterners in the U.S. are mainly Arabs, right? That depends on where you live. In the state of California, better than half are Iranian or Afghan; in Maryland, practically all are Iranian. Even if you restrict your attention to Americans of Arab origin, stereotypes quickly collapse. You would think it could at least be said with safety that they are mainly Muslims. Not so: more than three-quarters of Arab Americans are Christians. The principal Middle Eastern presence in my own town is St. Mark's Coptic Church. The Copts, who are Egyptian Christians, are certainly OMEA, and they speak Arabic for nonliturgical purposes, and have Arabic names. They have little reason to identify with Muslim terrorists, however, having been rudely persecuted by extremist Muslims in their homeland for decades. Misconceptions cut the other way, too. Care to guess what proportion of Muslim Americans are of Arab origins? Answer: around one in eight. Most American Muslims are black.

A Fallible but Useful Aid

That we could impose any even halfway reasonable system of "racial profiling" on this chaos seems impossible. Yet we can, where it matters most, and I believe we should; certainly in airport security, which, as a matter of fact, is where OMEA profiling began, during the hijack scares of the early 1970s. When boarding a plane, documents need to be presented, names declared, words exchanged. This gives security officials a much richer supply of data than a mere "eyeball" check. We return here to one of the points in another article that I have written on this subject, as affirmed by the U.S. Supreme Court: that "race"—which is to say, visible physical characteristics typical of, or at least frequent among, some group with a common origin—can be used as part of a suspect profile to identify targets for further investigation, provided there are other criteria in play.

We should profile at airports because, as the James Woods incident shows, profiling is an aid—very far from an infallible one, but still a useful one—to identifying those who want to harm us, in this as in any other area of law enforcement. To pretend that any person passing through airport security is as likely as any other to be a hijacker is absurd, just as it is absurd to pretend that any driver on the New Jersey Turnpike is as likely as any other to be transporting narcotics.

Crises like the present one can generate hysteria, it is true, but they can also have a clarifying effect on our outlook, sweeping away the wishful thinking of easier times, exposing the hollowness of relativism and moral equivalence, and forcing us to the main point. And peacetime has its own hysterias. I believe that when the long peace that ended on September 11 comes into perspective we shall see that the fuss about racial profiling was, ultimately, hysterical, driven by a dogmatic and unreasoned refusal to face up to group differences. So long as the authorities treat everyone with courtesy and apologize to the inconvenienced innocent, racial profiling is a practical and perfectly sensible tool for preventing crime and terrorism.

Chapter 4

How Should America Respond to Terrorism?

Chapter Preface

"Our war on terror is just beginning," stated President George W. Bush in his January 2002 State of the Union address. During the previous four months, in response to the September 11 attack, the United States had captured and arrested thousands of terrorists, destroyed terrorist training camps located in Afghanistan, and helped to liberate Afghanistan from the fundamentalist Taliban regime. However, at the beginning of 2002, terrorist instigator Osama bin Laden, as well as unknown numbers of his accomplices in the al-Qaeda terrorist network, remained at large. As the United States' inability to capture bin Laden illustrates, the war on terrorism is proving to be a difficult one. America's task is made more arduous by the fact that, as analysts maintain, the problem of terrorism extends far beyond the scope of bin Laden and al-Qaeda. For example, the U.S. government considers seven countries to be sponsors of terrorism or shelters for terrorist groups: Iran, Iraq, Syria, Libya, Sudan, North Korea, and Cuba. Of particular concern for the United States are Iran, Iraq, and North Korea—three countries that constitute what President Bush refers to as an "axis of evil"—because they are "hostile regimes" that are attempting to develop chemical, biological, and nuclear weapons of mass destruction.

Many analysts contend that military strikes against terrorists and terrorist-harboring nations provide the most effective response to attacks like the one that occurred on September 11. Most military strategists claim that bombing campaigns, such as the air strikes launched against targets in Afghanistan during late 2001, also offer a practical form of defense against future terrorism because they kill terrorists, interrupt communications among terrorist cells, destroy terrorist training sites, and disrupt the development of more sophisticated weapons. For example, during the early months of 2002, some analysts in the Bush administration suggested launching preemptive strikes against Iraq, arguing that Iraqi dictator Saddam Hussein had been developing weapons of mass destruction and posed a serious terrorist threat to America.

But some observers question the long-term effectiveness of military action against terrorism. While military power can deter the threat of war between countries, it has failed in deterring terrorist attacks, they maintain. And because military strikes inevitably kill innocent bystanders and civilians, they can feed the anger that provokes terrorism. Joyce Neu, executive director of the Joan B. Kroc Institute for Peace and Justice at the University of San Diego, argues that it is in the United States' best interests to respond to terrorism with restraint and magnanimity: "Children growing up in the developing world look to the developed world . . . as a model. Will Afghan and Iraqi children, having been subjected to hunger, disease, and oppression, look at the United States as a model of what they want for their country or as the enemy on whom to seek revenge? This is within our power to decide. Responding maganimously will sow the seeds of friendship; striking their homelands will give rise to a new generation of terrorists." Alternatives to military actions could include the promotion of education and economic development in poor nations and the establishment of an international criminal court to investigate and bring terrorists to justice.

The war on terrorism will likely be a long and sustained campaign. A fuller understanding of international relations, conflict resolution, and disaster preparedness will arm Americans with the information they need to help them face this long-term struggle. The following chapter presents further discussion on how the United States should respond to the September 11 attack and the threat of future terrorism.

Reject Violence and War as a Means of Resolving Conflict

by Howard Zinn

About the author: *Howard Zinn is a columnist for the* Progressive, *a monthly journal of left-wing opinion. He is also author of several books on politics and history, including* A People's History of the United States.

The images on television were heartbreaking: People on fire leaping to their deaths from a hundred stories up: people in panic racing from the scene in clouds of dust and smoke.

We knew there must be thousands of human beings buried under a mountain of debris. We could only imagine the terror among the passengers of the hijacked planes as they contemplated the crash, the fire, the end. Those scenes horrified and sickened me.

Then our political leaders came on television, and I was horrified and sickened again. They spoke of retaliation, of vengeance, of punishment.

We are at war, they said. And I thought: They have learned nothing, absolutely nothing, from the history of the twentieth century, from a hundred years of retaliation, vengeance, war, a hundred years of terrorism and counterterrorism, of violence met with violence in an unending cycle of stupidity.

We can all feel a terrible anger at whoever, in their insane idea that this would help their cause, killed thousands of innocent people. But what do we do with that anger? Do we react with panic, strike out violently and blindly just to show how tough we are? "We shall make no distinction," the President proclaimed, "between terrorists and countries that harbor terrorists."

So now we are bombing Afghanistan and inevitably killing innocent people because it is in the nature of bombing (and I say this as a former Air Force bombardier) to be indiscriminate, to "make no distinction." We are committing terrorism in order to "send a message" to terrorists.

The Old Way of Thinking

We have done that before. It is the old way of thinking, the old way of acting. It has never worked. Reagan bombed Libya, and Bush made war on Iraq, and Clinton bombed Afghanistan and also a pharmaceutical plant in the Sudan to "send a message" to terrorists. And then comes this horror in New York and Washington. Isn't it clear by now that sending a message to terrorists through violence doesn't work, that it only leads to more terrorism?

Haven't we learned anything from the Israeli-Palestinian conflict?

Car bombs planted by Palestinians bring air attacks and tanks by the Israeli government. That has been going on for years. It doesn't work.

And innocent people die on both sides.

> *"Isn't it clear by now that sending a message to terrorists through violence doesn't work, that it only leads to more terrorism?"*

Yes, it is an old way of thinking, and we need new ways. We need to think about the resentment all over the world felt by people who have been the victims of American military action.

In Vietnam, where we carried out terrorizing bombing attacks, using napalm and cluster bombs, on peasant villages.

In Latin America, where we supported dictators and death squads in Chile and El Salvador and Guatemala and Haiti.

In Iraq, where more than 500,000 children have died as a result of economic sanctions that the United States has insisted upon.

And, perhaps most important for understanding the current situation, in the occupied territories of the West Bank and Gaza, where a million and more Palestinians live under a cruel military occupation, while our government supplies Israel with high-tech weapons.

We need to imagine that the awful scenes of death and suffering we were witnessing on our television screens have been going on in other parts of the world for a long time, and only now can we begin to know what people have gone through, often as a result of our policies. We need to understand how some of those people will go beyond quiet anger to acts of terrorism.

That doesn't, by any means, justify the terror. Nothing justifies killing thousands of innocent people. But we would do well to see what might inspire such violence. And it will not be over until we stop concentrating on punishment and retaliation and think calmly and intelligently about how to address its causes.

We need new ways of thinking.

A $300 billion military budget has not given us security.

Military bases all over the world, our warships on every ocean, have not given us security.

Land mines and a "missile defense shield" will not give us security.

War Is Terrorism

We need to stop sending weapons to countries that oppress other people or their own people. We need to decide that we will not go to war, whatever reason is conjured up by the politicians or the media because war in our time is always indiscriminate, a war against innocents, a war against children.

War is terrorism, magnified a hundred times.

Yes, let's find the perpetrators of the awful acts of September 11. We must find the guilty parties and prosecute them. But we shouldn't engage in indiscriminate retaliation. When a crime is committed by someone who lives in a certain neighborhood, you don't destroy the neighborhood.

Yes, we can tend to immediate security needs. Let's take some of the billions allocated for "missile defense," totally useless against terrorist attacks such as this one, and pay the security people at airports decent wages and give them intensive training. Let's go ahead and hire marshals to be on every flight. But ultimately, there is no certain security against the unpredictable.

True, we can find bin Laden and his cohorts, or whoever were the perpetrators, and punish them. But that will not end terrorism so long as the pent-up grievances of decades, felt in so many countries in the Third World, remain unattended.

We cannot be secure so long as we use our national wealth for guns, warships, F-18s, cluster bombs, and nuclear weapons to maintain our position as a military superpower. We should use that wealth instead to become a moral superpower.

We must deal with poverty and sickness in other parts of the world where desperation breeds resentment. And here at home, our true security cannot come by putting the nation on a war footing, with all the accompanying threats to civil liberties that this brings. True security can come only when we use our resources to make us the model of a good society, prosperous and peacemaking, with free medical care for everyone, education and housing, guaranteed decent wages, and a clean environment for all. We cannot be secure by limiting our liberties, as some of our political leaders are demanding, but only by expanding them.

> *"We need to decide that we will not go to war . . . because war in our time is always indiscriminate, a war against innocents, a war against children."*

We should take our example not from our military and political leaders shouting "retaliate" and "war" but from the doctors and nurses and medical students and firefighters and police officers who were saving lives in the midst of mayhem, whose first thoughts were not violence but healing, not vengeance but compassion.

Engage in Military Retaliation Against Terrorists

by Stephen Cox

About the author: *Stephen Cox is a senior editor of* Liberty, *a monthly libertarian review of thought, culture, and politics.*

At the climax of the last book of the Bible, the book of Revelation, St. John presents his vision of the end of history:

> And I John saw the holy city, new Jerusalem, coming down from God out of heaven, prepared as a bride adorned for her husband. And I heard a great voice out of heaven saying, Behold, the tabernacle of God is with men . . . and God shall wipe away all tears from their eyes; and there shall be no more death, neither sorrow, nor crying, neither shall there be any more pain; for the former things are passed away.

For two thousand years, this vision has inspired the devout and amused the skeptical. But no one, until now, ever thought that the event had already taken place.

No one, until now, ever thought that he was actually living in a world like the New Jerusalem, where pain and sorrow and death had become, well, obsolete. Only in the aftermath of the apocalyptic destruction of the World Trade Center has this mighty truth dawned upon the consciousness of a minority—but a significant minority—of Western intellectuals.

To these people (are you one of them?), the way to deal with the atrocity of September 11 is, basically, to ignore it. Yes, they admit that it happened. It was "shocking." It was "horrifying." They "grieve for the victims." But for them, terrorism still has an air of unreality. They see no necessity for the United States to engage in military retaliation. Quite the contrary. They believe that the terrorists will stop, if the United States does. They believe that America's enemies have good reasons for theft enmity, and that it is up to America, therefore, to "end the cycle of violence." That means dropping the arrogant assumption that we have the right to punish foreign nations for the ("alleged") misdeeds of their residents. If we want to end terrorist attacks, we should look "beyond the horror of September 11" and think about how we can find nonviolent solutions to international problems.

The Peace and Justice Crowd

Sounds good, doesn't it? Certainly it sounds good to the "signers and j'iners," the people who busy themselves sending out petitions for "justice, not revenge" and other self-evidently worthy causes. When they speak of peace and reason and cooperation, their satisfaction—indeed their self-satisfaction—always appears complete. Eloquent about the risks of war, they seem certain that nothing in their own proposals could possibly entail a risk. They appear certain, in other words, that they are already living in the New Jerusalem, in that blessed place where morality and practicality are, at last, one and the same, that place where there is no longer any necessity for death, neither sorrow, nor crying. To inhabit that risk-free world, all we need to do is to live, as St. John puts it, "in the Spirit."

> *"At best, [the anti-anti-terrorist attitude] expresses a true idealism about peace and justice. At worst, it expresses a cruel disregard for reality."*

It's interesting that nobody except Americans ever seems to reason in this way. Sure, there are zealots and thugs and morons all over the world who are willing to riot for "peace" at a moment's notice, but they know that the peace they seek can only be purchased at the price of destruction, the destruction not just of America's foreign alliances, military bases, and so forth, but also of American capitalism and any other identifiably American aspect of world culture. It's only Americans who get so carried away by evangelical beliefs as to imagine, not merely that everyone ought to be traveling toward that City on the Hill, but that everyone ought to act as if the journey had actually been completed.

I'm as vulnerable to the evangelical spirit as any other American. I always want to believe that we are half a mile from the New Jerusalem, and getting there fast. I have very strong isolationist and peace-freak proclivities. Nevertheless, even I know that the anti-anti-terrorist attitude is bunk. At best, it expresses a true idealism about peace and justice. At worst, it expresses a cruel disregard for reality.

Discouraging the Wicked Witches

This disregard achieves fantastic proportions in the idea that, pending judicial proceedings, no one should be "punished" for the September 11 atrocity. After all, it is said, we haven't seen all the evidence against Osama bin Laden. He may be guilty of nothing more than *saying* that he wants to have us all killed, riling up a few mobs here and there, running a few boot camps for weekend warriors, and, from time to time, blowing up a ship or an embassy somewhere. In sum, he may be little more than an "ideological role model" for the people who are trying to kill us.

Yes, I can see it now: Dorothy and her friends are walking along through Oz when, suddenly, the flying monkeys descend, abducting the girl and leaving her friends for dead. Well, who really knows who was responsible? True, the Wicked Witch showed up before, and made some threats—but maybe she was joking. Maybe she was just carried away by her own rhetoric. And, true, the flying monkeys are known to be allied with her—but maybe she didn't actually direct their attack. Remember, we have only the word of the Wizard that she is the focus of evil, and the Wizard has been known to lie. Clearly, no water should be poured on the Witch until she is arrested and tried at The Hague.

Sorry. She's a wicked witch, and she has to be killed. That will discourage the other wicked witches. And you can see what miraculous effects this kind of thing can have on a gang of flying monkeys. Once she was dead, all they could think of to say was, "Hail, Dorothy!"

A Convenient Theory

At this point, however, we should consider the assumption of many leftist and (I am sorry to say) libertarian experts on the New Jerusalem, to the effect that America would have no enemies in the Muslim world if it didn't insist on interfering with the Muslim world. A corollary assumption is the belief that American vengeance for the victims of September 11 will "only produce even worse reprisals." Let me reduce these assumptions to even plainer language. The idea is this: If Americans would simply cease to be *bad*, then everybody else would very naturally and irresistibly start being *good*.

This is, at least, a very *convenient* theory. If you are a pacifist, it is very *convenient* for you to believe, not only that war is evil, but also that war will never work. If you are an isolationist, it is very *convenient* for you to believe, not only that foreign interventions are always wrong, but also that foreign interventions are always counterproductive. In fact, however, morality and practicality are not always the same. They are two clearly distinguishable things. That's why they are called by two different names, and why it is so hard to think about either one of them without thinking about its difference from the other. Even a murder can have good effects; even the noblest act of heroism can have bad ones. Everybody knows this, except when the talk turns to politics.

> *"America's chronic involvement in foreign disputes is . . . an evil. Unfortunately, even worse evils would follow if we beat a precipitate retreat from our foreign involvements."*

War is an evil. I believe that America's chronic involvement in foreign disputes is also an evil. Unfortunately, even worse evils would follow if we beat a precipitate retreat from our foreign involvements. (Please do not tell me that you decline to choose the lesser of the two evils. You have no other choice—unless you think that you really, truly do have the option of living in the New Jerusalem, right here, right now.) Our withdrawal from foreign alliances would offer us no more protection than President McKinley got

> *"Any weakness we show at this point would only invite further aggression."*

from the fact that he was not the Tsar of Russia. McKinley was assassinated by a terrorist to whom that slight difference of identity did not appear important. From the terrorist's point of view, Nicholas II and William McKinley were significant simply because they were both enemies of the social revolution. From the point of view of people like Osama bin Laden, liberal civilization is the enemy, and every aspect of liberal civilization—from women's equality to the disgustingly permissive Saudi royal family—is as appalling and hateful as the presence of American marines in the Middle East.

Does anyone really think that if America withdrew from all its alliances today, the international terrorist movement would suspend military operations and devote itself to seeking KFC franchises and erecting statues to George W. Bush? Not hardly. Any weakness we show at this point would only invite further aggression. If America yielded and withdrew from all forward positions in the Middle East (as I wish that America would do, when America decides to do it on its own), America would simply be confronted with a new series of demands, culminating, I suppose, in a demand to withdraw from Dearborn, Mich.

Speaking Practically

The question of whether, and to what degree, American policies "provoked" the events of September 11 is interesting in certain respects, but it is not interesting in respect to our plans for the future. Adolf Hitler may have come to power because of the injustices of the Treaty of Versailles, but once he came to power, abrogation of the Treaty by Britain and France would not have kept him out of war. In fact, the Treaty was dead as soon as he marched his troops into the demilitarized zone of western Germany, three and a half years before the beginning of World War II.

The claims that bin Laden & Co. make on reality are actually somewhat larger and less easily satisfied than the claims that Hitler made. I don't mean to suggest that the Islamic terrorists are more possessed of evil than Hitler was; that's a question of morality, and right now, I'm talking practicality. Hitler wanted to create a certain social order in Germany and some of its surroundings; he specifically disavowed any messianic desire to spread Nazism beyond the borders of Germania. Terrorism, however, has long operated without even this modest degree of ideological discretion. Nihilists and anarchists and the other social revolutionaries of the 19th century weren't about to be fobbed off with little concessions like the abolition of serfdom; it was the Tsar who abolished serfdom who perished by a terrorist's bomb. Now the reactionaries of the Islamic world demand that, pending Western evacuation of Arabia, all (male) infidels be killed, wherever found. Do you think that ambitions like theirs can be satisfied by a pullout from Arabia? And do you think that people who enjoyed massacring thousands in New York City wouldn't get even more fun out of an atom bomb?

No, we are not living in the New Jerusalem. If you believe we are, you should take another look at those demonstrations of terrorist supporters in places like Pakistan and Afghanistan. That quadrant of the Holy City seems to be inhabited exclusively by angry young males (or, perhaps, one very angry young male, surrounded by a lot of mirrors), males who appear to be occupied exclusively in screaming, surging, and pillaging. An odd note is the grinning happiness shown by the AYMs whenever a Western camera starts pointing in their direction. You remember the communist tendency toward doublethink? It didn't die with communism. These people think that everything in the West is evil, except the products that they happen to have a use for—products that they love and cherish, as if they could have the products without the culture. They can't; their revolt is the revolt of the parasite. Yet for that very reason it is insatiably envious, incapable, on its own, of facing any essential truth about either itself or its enemy.

> *"There's no reason to imagine that terrorism will simply starve on the vine once America stops subsidizing it."*

It may be that the West has helped to fuel this revolt by its feckless charity and search for friends. The isolationists have much to teach us about how that works; their arguments, in this department, are often cogent indeed. But there's no reason to imagine that terrorism will simply starve on the vine once America stops subsidizing it. The terrorists will get their camo fatigues from someone else. Perhaps, eventually, they may even learn how to make their own.

How to Defeat Terrorism

So where do we go from here? There are three things that are capable of defeating terrorism.

The first, and potentially the most conclusive, is boredom. The terrorist movements of the late 19th century eventually fizzled out—partly, it seems, because the terrorists got bored with plotting to assassinate people. Some of them changed their political tactics; others, it seems, just grew up. Unfortunately, however, some of them kept at it, like the terrorists who started World War I; and it will never be known how many would have institutionalized themselves permanently, like the Irish Republican Army, if they had not been the targets of repressive measures.

The second means of defeating terrorism is, therefore, direct repression of the terrorists. Every dead terrorist is a terrorist who will never commit another act of terror. Sorry, peace dude: Violence often works. As to the idea that repression "creates martyrs," "sows dragon's teeth," "fuels more rage," and so forth . . . sometimes it does, but in this case, who cares? Maybe Osama bin Laden's untimely death will be avenged by a bunch of yahoos who decide to blow up the World Trade Center. Oops! that already happened. The terrorists were already fueled with enough rage to do that. Do you think that if we don't pursue bin Laden, they're going to say to themselves, "Oh, I guess we shouldn't blow up the Chrysler Building, after all." I don't think so. But if America's war on bin Laden is successful, some of them will say (to themselves), "Dude! That coulda been me. I think I'm gonna go back to Florida State and pick up that degree in computer science."

The third means is an attack on terrorist states. That's the approach that President Ronald Reagan took when he bombed Libya. Until then, Libya was a focus of terrorist activity. Now it's not. Why? We repressed Libya. We shouldn't be under any illusions about terrorism being a strictly spontaneous overflow of powerful feeling. Abou ben Adhemr, age 18, native of Taliban City, Talibanistan, may be as mad as hell about America's squishing of his hero, Osama bin Laden, but he will probably be in no position to avenge the death, so long as he's unable to locate people who are well-organized and well-funded enough to help him. The trouble starts when he hooks up with some government-protected agency that gives him money and sanctuary and all the other stuff he needs to live as a professional terrorist with some prospect of a dramatic success. That's why America should do what it can to put terrorist states out of business.

Now, it's obvious, simply from the fact that we do *not* live in the New Jerusalem, that we have no guarantee that any of these three means of ending terrorism will totally succeed. There's no guarantee of total success in anything. But there are guarantees of failure. "Mr. bin Laden, we're really upset with you. We're going to investigate this situation, and if we find evidence that will stand up in court, we are going to insist that the government of Afghanistan extradite you to New York, where you will be given a fair trial and be either convicted or acquitted. As to force and coercion, we're not going to stoop to your level. Meanwhile, we're going to appoint a committee, headed by the Rev. Jesse Jackson, to review the question of Why People Who Hate Capitalism and Liberalism Also Hate America." That's what I'd call a guarantee of practical failure.

A Moral View

But let's take a strictly moral view of the situation. There are very few people, even radical libertarians, who would deny that the American government has a duty to pursue and punish any gang of Americans who murder thousands of people for the purpose of emphasizing their own religious views. The legitimate purpose of the state, if any, is the protection of liberty and property. But if the state has the duty to go after a gang of Americans, is there any moral reason why it can't go after a gang of non-Americans who do the same thing? What? Does morality change at the border? Is there some reason to believe that the border of Afghanistan is more sacred than life, liberty, and property?

No, what's wrong with war is the prospect of people being shot, bombed, crushed, crippled, burned alive. That's why war is bad—not because it takes place on somebody else's soil, instead of our own. The war that America is in right now began on America's soil on September 11, 2001. It will continue on America's soil, indeed it will escalate, until (1) the terrorists get bored; (2) we get to the terrorists and kill them; (3) we take action against the states that support them and either neutralize or kill them, too. The first option is, unluckily, outside our power to implement. The second and third options seem to lie within our power.

> *"Every dead terrorist is a terrorist who will never commit another act of terror. Sorry, peace dude: Violence often works."*

Isn't it remarkable? In combating international terrorism, the United States government is doing one of the few things that it has a clear and legitimate power to do. And that's precisely what critics of the anti-terrorist campaign don't want it to do. They are good people, many of them. Their critiques of government, in other contexts, have often been extremely valuable. Now, however, they are doing little more than identifying themselves as politically irrelevant, and that is a shame and a loss.

There's another passage of Bible prophecy that speaks of this. It's in the sixth chapter of Jeremiah, and it's much more realistic than the Bible passage with which I started. Speaking of certain intellectuals of his time, Jeremiah says, "They have healed also the hurt of my people slightly, saying, Peace, peace: when there is no peace."

Hold a National Conversation on Foreign Policy

by Mike Miller

About the author: *Mike Miller is editor of* Social Policy, *a quarterly journal that examines politics and strategies for community organizing.*

We Americans revealed the best of our character during and after the September 11 attack. Priorities changed. People are reaching out to friends, neighbors, strangers and "The Other". Americans—native born and immigrants, here legally and otherwise—continue to generously give their time, blood and money. Everyday people acted heroically. Sports commentators said they need a term other than "hero" for baseball stars. We've come a long way since our World War II internment of Japanese-Americans, and we still have a way to go. But for every despicable anti-Arab/anti-Muslim act, there are laudable stories of people reaching out to and protecting Muslim neighbors, co-workers and store-front business people. At our best, this is who we are as a people.

In this tragedy and horror there is an opportunity. The fact of "globalization" is now on everyone's mind. So is the desire to talk about it. The country has been instantly politicized. Everyday Americans are asking, "Why do they hate us?" This is a time for a national conversation on our role in the world. The conversation needs to be reflective, patient, deliberative, compassionate, tough-minded and open-ended in character. It should take place in civil society, unmediated by the filter of sound-bites or banal posturings in what TV simple-mindedly calls "right" vs. "left" debates. We have at hand an opportunity to offer real alternatives to a people struggling to discover what it means to be citizens of a world power. We must not lose this opportunity. It is time for a proactive strategy to define the terms of the foreign policy debate in the 2002 and 2004 national elections.

Challenging People to Accept Responsibility

There are two initial obstacles to having this conversation—the Executive Branch's encroachments on the Constitution and the common belief among Americans that they are not competent to discuss politics, especially foreign policy.

We need to convince Americans that they are competent to make foreign policy decisions. Americans are uncertain of their role in foreign policy formulation. Too often, they think it is a matter for "experts" and that to question the experts is unpatriotic. The core of democratic faith is that the people shall be sovereign, that given the opportunity they will more often than not make the best decisions. But the opportunity won't be given to us; we have to fight for it. The most patriotic thing we can do is accept the responsibility our form of government demands.

Americans are also unclear on the issue of secrecy. Too often they confuse policy with implementation.

> *"This is a time for a national conversation on our role in the world."*

Congress and the American people could have debated the question of whether we should be bombing Afghanistan. That is a policy question. Answering it doesn't mean revealing the types of planes to be used, their departure points, dates of attack or any other matters of implementation. Open debate and security can both be preserved. The Congress has abdicated its Constitutional responsibility, and the Administration is pressing it to relinquish more. The President is Commander in Chief, not King. Nowhere does the Constitution say the people shall rule except in matters of foreign policy.

The most trusted institutions in our nation are our religious ones. This editorial is a call to the religious community to initiate a national conversation, to lead a process of deliberation and discernment, on America's role in the world. The religious community can invite other groups in civil society to join it in this discussion. Unions, professional associations, neighborhood organizations and others should take part.

Another major forum for such discussions is the classrooms of America, beginning at the kindergarten level where respect for other peoples and faiths must be taught. Middle- and high-school students can begin to learn that as adults their votes will have to, in part, express their views on foreign policy matters. The country's teacher unions and parent organizations should press school districts to create classroom and field visit opportunities for students to engage in this discussion. In many places this will require a struggle over the very definitions of "democracy" and "patriotism." It is a struggle worth waging.

The people of the country must begin the long, hard task of entering foreign policy debates as participants, not spectators. Over the past 25 years, community organizing has developed a method for effective democratic participation. This approach calls for a different understanding and practice of leadership.

Traditionally, leaders adopt policy then "educate" followers or members on the efficacy of what they did. Too often, the result is alienation in the pews or the ranks. In this different approach, leaders engage members in asking the questions. When people own the questions they will be committed to the answers that they themselves find. In community organizing, large numbers of people, coming from a wide range of views, meet to define problems and seek solutions. They meet with policy makers and experts. They publicly expose and take direct action against those who refuse to meet or who give evasive answers. In a conversation on America's role in the world, people with "hawkish" and "dovish" sympathies, as well as those who aren't sure, should be in on the ground floor of framing the questions. They should meet public and private policy makers and experts and ask specific and pointed questions. We can use this method to hold public officials and corporate executives accountable to the public interest on foreign policy matters.

Within community organizations using this approach, the people apply a careful process of deliberation and discernment to answers to their questions. More often than not, consensus or near-consensus emerges as more and more information is gathered and evaluated. The good sense and sound judgment of most people triumph over slogans and shibboleths. The organization adopts the policies that will guide it in negotiations with power structure decision makers. And if these negotiations don't bring desired results, the people

> *"The President is Commander in Chief, not King. Nowhere does the Constitution say the people shall rule except in matters of foreign policy."*

take direct action. Every community in the country has organizers who know how to teach the skills of this process. The spirit of civic caring and social responsibility that emerged from the terrorists' attacks can guide the discussion.

Redefining the Terms of the Debate

This approach works for all open-minded people of good will. What are the possible outcomes of such a conversation?

Most people now take one of two positions:

- War is the way to security and peace.
- Peace (some add justice in our treatment of other countries) must be substituted for war.

How are we to appraise each of these alternatives?

- The first, now dominating our nation's strategy, says, "America must wage war on the terrorists, and the countries that sponsor them. They must be destroyed if there is to be security and peace."
- The second says, "peace is the answer; get at the root causes of terrorism by acting justly in the world."
- There is a third possibility: War, Justice, Peace and Security (in no particular

order). Diplomatic, political, legal and police action are needed to eliminate the terrorist cells that now exist around the world. Economic sanctions and military action may be required against states sponsoring terrorism. Economic, political and social justice must guide American foreign policy in its relations with other peoples and nations throughout the world so that conditions breeding converts to terrorism are eliminated. Peace must include security for all nations and peoples, and their right to democratic self-determination.

A new timeline is needed. The strategic problem is to frame the questions for a new conversation in a way that most Americans will understand and accept. Out of this conversation, a different framing of the issue can and will arise. It can determine how the foreign policy debate is conducted in the future elections. It is toward these elections that a proactive strategy should be aimed. It will take that long; the time is worth spending.

Prepare for a Sustained Conflict

by David Aaron

About the author: *David Aaron served as deputy national security advisor during the 1979 Iran hostage crisis in which fifty-two Americans were held for fourteen months. He is a senior national adviser at Dorsey and Whitney LLP in Washington, D.C.*

It was not about us; it was about them. That is the thing to understand about the September 11 terrorist attack on the World Trade Center and the Pentagon.

Many motives may have figured in the minds of those who directed this atrocity. Perhaps they hate us, as some pundits say, because we are rich, or because of our liberal and secular culture, or because of our support for Israel—but none of these reasons is fundamental. The basic objective of the terrorists is to destroy the Middle Eastern governments that are friendly to the West and replace them with radical Islamic regimes. Osama bin Laden has said that the U.S. military presence in the Middle East, particularly in Saudi Arabia, defiles Islam and is justification for jihad. Though cloaked in the language of religion, this comes close to the heart of the matter. Bin Laden and company want to see their version of Islam dominate the Arab world, if not the entire Islamic world. As President George W. Bush said to the joint session of Congress, we happen to be in the way.

Certainly the grievances of the Palestinians are a rallying point exploited by extremists and terrorists of many stripes. But it is nonsense to assert, as King Abdullah II of Jordan has, that the tragedy in this country would not have happened if only Israel and Palestine had reached a peace agreement in the year 2000. Moves toward peace have always provoked more terrorism, not less. Moreover, the operation that culminated on September 11, 2001, was under way for years.

The radical Islamic movement is born of the failure of much of the Muslim Arab world to modernize. Arab socialism as a path to modernity reached a dead end in the tyranny of Saddam Hussein, and Arab nationalism proved equally barren. The corrupt elites that control the government and the economy of many countries have squandered oil riches and left the Arab masses in grinding poverty. Nowhere in the Arab world are there real democracies.

For some Muslims—often middle-class or privileged ones—the failure of their societies is unbearable. And rather than blame themselves, they look to external causes and seek solace in religion. The response of a few is to try to return to a 10th century of their imagination in search of a fundamentalist, militant, even apocalyptic Islam that has never existed. It matters not that acts of terror and suicide are antithetical to Islamic tenets.

The Need for Measured Retaliation

The strategy of those who perpetrated this attack on America is to provoke a U.S. response that they can represent as a holy war against Islam, thus gaining additional recruits and undermining the legitimacy of moderate Arab states that cooperate with us. No one questions that retaliation is essential; the perpetrators and their supporters cannot be allowed to get off scot-free. But the retaliation must be measured and discreet, or we may drive more people into the arms of the extremists and also lose the enormous sympathy and support the tragedy has generated for us around the world. The Bush administration seems fully aware of this trap but finds it difficult to avoid.

While the president has sensibly counseled patience, his rhetoric has raised expectations to unrealistic levels: "The enemy is terrorism itself." Our aim is to "root out terrorism everywhere." This is an impossible objective. Are we going to go after the Irish Republican Army (IRA) and its agents in the United States? How about Basque separatists? We have no dog in that fight. Or the Tamil Tigers? Sikhs of Kashmir? Chechens? The Kurds in Turkey or—closer to home—the Zapatistas in Mexico? No, we are not. By the time he spoke to Congress, the president had qualified his language. We are now targeting "terrorists of global reach."

Even so, we will have to be painfully discriminating. Radical and terrorist organizations in the Middle East often help one another, even across ideological lines. Besides al-Qaeda, are we going to take on Hezbollah, Islamic Jihad, Hamas, the Muslim Brotherhood, and the various

> *"No one questions that retaliation is essential. . . . But the retaliation must be measured and discreet, or we may drive more people into the arms of the extremists."*

Algerian terrorist groups? Some of them, such as Hamas, are directly engaged in the Israeli-Palestinian struggle. Are we going to become combatants in that conflict? Not a good idea if our strategic goal is to defend moderate Arab states against a radical Islamic takeover.

Aside from protecting our people, every action we take must be measured against the goal of thwarting the control and domination of the Middle East by Islamic radicals—and enhancing the survival of states that are willing to cooperate with the West. Retaliation, capturing terrorist leaders, destroying safe havens—all of this must support and be subordinate to that overarching objective.

Will we prevail? The answer to that is all about us and not about them. Despite the outpouring of patriotism, many commentators have questioned whether Americans have the attention span to pursue the long, horizonless war we have declared. But the problem goes far beyond our collective attention-deficit disorder. We are ill prepared, psychologically and perhaps even militarily, for the kind of war that must be waged.

The Lessons of Vietnam

The September 11 attacks have frequently been compared to Pearl Harbor. As a wake-up call, certainly. For the struggle ahead, however, Vietnam provides a much closer analogy as well as an object lesson.

First, there is the danger of "Americanizing" the conflict with Islamic radicals. When the United States moved into Vietnam in force, it turned a struggle among the Vietnamese into one with America. Apart from Israel, the battle against Islamic radicals has largely been waged within such countries as Saudi Arabia, Egypt, Algeria, and Syria. In order to thwart bin Laden's efforts to turn these inter-Arab struggles into a war between America and Islam, we must depend on our friends in the Middle East to bear the principal burden in this fight.

> *"Every action we take must be measured against the goal of thwarting the control and domination of the Middle East by Islamic radicals."*

The United States can supplement its intelligence capabilities, provide material support and training, and perhaps even conduct special military operations on a selective basis. But we must take care not to undermine the political legitimacy of the moderate Arab governments, or they could fall from within as we defend them from without.

Second, there is the problem of finding the enemy. The Vietcong hid in the jungle, in tunnels, in sanctuaries in Cambodia and Laos, and among the people. Despite massive defoliation, saturation bombing, incursions into Cambodia and Laos, and prodigious intelligence efforts, we seldom found them. Similarly, Islamic terrorists hide in the mountains, operate from sanctuary states, and move invisibly among the Arab people. Identifying them will require better intelligence, but the information will infrequently rise to the standard of certainty. Rooting them out, therefore, will inevitably involve killing the innocent and those only peripherally involved. Does America have the stomach for what in Latin America is called a "dirty war"?

Third, there is the question of sanctuaries. In the Vietnam War, we bombed but never invaded North Vietnam, the principal sanctuary. Will we need to invade Afghanistan in order to depose the Taliban and chase the terrorists from their havens? As the Russians amply demonstrated, this would be a massive undertaking. [The United States began bombing Afghanistan in October 2001.] And what of Iraq, Syria, Libya, and Iran, all of which harbor and support terrorists? If they do not respond positively to the lesson being readied for Afghanistan, can we—will we—invade them all? Neither the U.S. military nor the American people are ready for war on such a scale.

"This war is fully justified by our strategic interests. Despite daunting obstacles, it is by no means doomed to failure."

We might try to bomb the sanctuary countries into acquiescence. It worked in Yugoslavia but, unfortunately, not in Vietnam or anyplace else. Iraq is just the most recent example of how a bombing campaign alone will probably only strengthen the control of the targeted regime. And the likely civilian destruction will radicalize more people throughout the region.

The fourth lesson of Vietnam concerns the corrosive effect on popular support of what is now called "asymmetric warfare." The small victories that characterized the conflict in Vietnam were hard to measure and uninspiring. Our government had to resort to the infamous "body count" to show any semblance of military success. The defeats were seen on TV in America's living rooms and were psychologically devastating.

The battle with terrorist organizations will be even more frustrating. Capturing or killing Osama bin Laden would be satisfying but would not necessarily stop acts of terror against us. U.S. victories against terrorist cells will be small affairs and often kept secret to preserve intelligence assets and protect our Middle East allies from adverse public reaction. So other than our initial retaliation, there may be little to put on television to show that we are winning.

On the other hand, our defeats—and we must expect defeats despite all our efforts—may again involve massive loss of American lives and be displayed on television for everyone to see. This "asymmetric" impact will test Americans' resolve as never before.

Over the Long Haul

Finally, against this backdrop of operational difficulty and potential public frustration, we need to consider whether the American people will support this fight over the long haul. Vietnam offers no guidance in this respect since we were never attacked at home. Indeed, it is sobering to realize that the fatalities inflicted on Americans in one day, September 11, amount to more than 10 percent of American deaths in a decade of combat in Vietnam.

Naturally, we want to fight back because we have been attacked. But once the initial round of retaliation is completed, will the public remain steadfast? In the

Gulf War, we fought for the principle that aggression shall not stand; but we were also fighting over oil, and that became controversial. A quick and almost painless victory silenced such criticism. Now we will be fighting for the principle that terrorism will not be tolerated—and to preempt a future and worse conflict between the West and a radical Islamic Middle East. But oil is not irrelevant to our interests in the region. In a long, drawn-out campaign against terrorism, this could become a source of doubt in the eyes of many Americans.

Perhaps this is why the president has reached back to the rhetoric of the Cold War and said that we are fighting for freedom. This also is an eerie echo of Vietnam. And freedom is hardly what friendly Arab governments seek under the circumstances.

This war is fully justified by our strategic interests. Despite daunting obstacles, it is by no means doomed to failure; America has enormous resources and worldwide support. We must conduct the war, however, in a way that ensures that this support—above all, on the home front—remains strong. The administration needs to start by being candid; this, too, is a lesson of Vietnam. We may be able to disrupt the terrorists' operations, keep them on the run, neutralize their key leaders, undermine the governments that provide sanctuary—in short, we should be able to control and minimize the level of Islamic terrorism—but it seems unlikely that it can be eliminated entirely.

Can we sustain our commitment in such a struggle? Can the generation scarred by Vietnam accept the casualties and moral compromises that the battle against terror inevitably entails? Can the subsequent generations of Americans who have little or no knowledge of the Vietnam War learn its hard lessons? If so, we can prevail.

It's all about us.

Dismantle the International Terror Network

by Benjamin Netanyahu

About the author: *Benjamin Netanyahu served as Israeli prime minister from 1996 to 1999.*

What is at stake today is nothing less than the survival of our civilization. There may be some who would have thought a week ago [in early September 2001] that to talk in these apocalyptic terms about the battle against international terrorism was to engage in reckless exaggeration. No longer.

Each one of us today understands that we are all targets, that our cities are vulnerable, and that our values are hated with an unmatched fanaticism that seeks to destroy our societies and our way of life. I am certain that I speak on behalf of my entire nation [of Israel] when I say: Today, we are all Americans—in grief, as in defiance.

In grief, because my people have faced the agonizing horrors of terror for many decades, and we feel an instant kinship with both the victims of this tragedy and the great nation that mourns its fallen brothers and sisters.

In defiance, because just as my country continues to fight terrorism in our battle for survival, I know that America will not cower before this challenge.

I have absolute confidence that if we, the citizens of the free world, led by President [George W.] Bush, marshal the enormous reserves of power at our disposal, harness the steely resolve of a free people, and mobilize our collective will, we shall eradicate this evil from the face of the earth.

But to achieve this goal, we must first, however, answer several questions: Who is responsible for this terrorist onslaught? Why? What is the motive behind these attacks? And most importantly, what must be done to defeat these evil forces?

Terrorist States

The first and most crucial thing to understand is this: There is no international terrorism without the support of sovereign states. International terrorism simply

From "A Wake-Up Call from Hell," by Benjamin Netanyahu, *American Legion Magazine*, November 2001.

cannot be sustained for long without the regimes that aid and abet it.

Terrorists are not suspended in mid-air. They train, arm and indoctrinate their killers from within safe havens on territory provided by terrorist states. Often these regimes provide the terrorists with intelligence, money and operational assistance, dispatching them to serve as deadly proxies to wage a hidden war against more powerful enemies.

These regimes mount a worldwide propaganda campaign to legitimize terror, besmirching its victims and exculpating its practitioner . . . Iran, Libya and Syria call the United States and Israel racist countries that

> *"Take away . . . state support, and the entire scaffolding of international terrorism will collapse into the dust."*

abuse human rights? Even Orwell could not have imagined such a world.

Take away all this state support, and the entire scaffolding of international terrorism will collapse into the dust.

The international terrorist network is thus based on regimes—Iran, Iraq, Syria, Taliban Afghanistan, Yasser Arafat's Palestinian Authority and several other Arab regimes such as the Sudan. These regimes are the ones that harbor the terrorist groups: Osama bin Laden in Afghanistan, Hizballah and others in Syrian-controlled Lebanon, Hamas, Islamic Jihad and the recently mobilized Fatah and Tanzim factions in the Palestinian territories, and sundry other terror organizations based in such capitals as Damascus, Baghdad and Khartoum. These terrorist states and terror organizations together form a terror network, whose constituent parts support each other operationally as well as politically.

For example, the Palestinian groups cooperate closely with Hizballah, which in turn links them to Syria, Iran and bin Laden. These offshoots of terror have affiliates in other states that have not yet uprooted their presence, such as Egypt, Yemen and Saudi Arabia.

The Growth of Islamic Terrorism

Now, how did this come about?

The growth of this terror network is the result of several developments in the last two decades: Chief among them is the Khomeini Revolution and the establishment of a clerical Islamic state in Iran. This created a sovereign spiritual base for fomenting a strident Islamic militancy worldwide—a militancy that was often backed by terror. Equally important was the victory in the Afghan war of the international mujaheedin brotherhood.

This international band of zealots, whose ranks include Osama bin Laden, saw their victory over the Soviet Union as providential proof of the innate supremacy of faithful Moslems over the weak infidel powers. They believed that even the superior weapons of a superpower could not withstand their superior will.

To this should also be added Saddam Hussein's escape from destruction at the end of the Gulf War, his dismissal of U.N. [weapons] monitors and his growing confidence that he can soon develop unconventional weapons to match those of the west.

Finally, the creation of Yasser Arafat's terror enclave gave a safe haven to militant Islamic terrorist groups such as Hamas and Islamic Jihad. Like their mujaheedin cousins, they drew inspiration from Israel's hasty withdrawal from Lebanon, glorified as a great Moslem victory by the Syrian-backed Hizballah. Under Arafat's rule, these Palestinian Islamic terrorist groups made repeated use of the technique of suicide bombing, going so far as to run summer camps in Gaza that teach Palestinian children how to become suicide martyrs.

Here is what Arafat's government-controlled newspaper, *Al Hayat Al Jadida*, said on September 11, the very day of the suicide bombing of the World Trade Center and the Pentagon: "The suicide bombers of today are the noble successors of the Lebanese suicide bombers, who taught the U.S. Marines a tough lesson in (Lebanon) . . . These suicide bombers are the salt of the earth, the engines of history . . . They are the most honorable people among us . . ."

A simple rule prevails here: The success of terrorists in one part of the terror network emboldens terrorists throughout the network. This then is the who.

Anti-Western Hostility

Now for the why: Though its separate parts may have local objectives and take part in local conflicts, the main motivation driving the terror network is an anti-western hostility that seeks to achieve nothing less than a reversal of history. It seeks to roll back the west and install an extremist form of Islam as the dominant power in the world.

It seeks to do this not by means of its own advancement and progress, but by destroying the enemy. This hatred is the product of a seething resentment that has simmered for centuries in certain parts of the Arab and Islamic world.

> *"The success of terrorists in one part of the terror network emboldens terrorists throughout the network."*

Most Moslems in the world, including the vast majority of the growing Moslem communities in the west, are not guided by this interpretation of history, nor are they moved by its call for a holy war against the west.

But some are. And though their numbers are small compared to the peaceable majority, they nevertheless constitute a growing hinterland for this militancy.

Militant Islamists resented the west for pushing back the triumphant march of Islam into the heart of Europe many centuries ago. Its adherents, believing in the innate supremacy of Islam, then suffered a series of shocks when in the last two centuries that same hated, supposedly inferior west penetrated Islamic realms in North Africa, the Middle East and the Persian Gulf. For them the mission was clear: The west had to be first pushed out of these areas. Pro-western middle eastern regimes were toppled in rapid succession, including in Iran.

And Israel, the Middle East's only democracy and its purest manifestation of western progress and freedom, must be wiped off the face of the earth. Thus, the soldiers of militant Islam do not hate the west because of Israel; they hate Israel because of the west—because they see it is an island of western democratic values in a Moslem-Arab sea of despotism. That is why they call Israel the "Little Satan," to distinguish it clearly from the country that has always been and will always be the "Great Satan"—the United States of America.

Nothing better illustrates this than Osama bin Laden's call for Jihad against the United States in 1998. He gave as his primary reason not Israel, not the Palestinians, not the peace process, but rather the very presence of the United States "occupying the land of Islam in the holiest of places."

And where is that?

"The Arabian peninsula," says bin Laden, where America is "plundering its riches, dictating to its rulers and humiliating its people."

Israel, by the way, comes a distant third, after "the continuing aggression against the Iraqi people." (*Al Quds al Arabi*—Feb. 23, 1998). For the bin Ladens of the world Israel is merely a sideshow. America is the target.

Destroying America

But re-establishing a resurgent Islam requires not just rolling back the west; it requires destroying its main engine, the United States. And if the United States cannot be destroyed just now, it can be first humiliated—as in the Tehran hostage crisis two decades ago—and then ferociously attacked again and again, until it is brought to its knees.

But the ultimate goal remains the same: Destroy America and win eternity.

Some of you may find it hard to believe that Islamic militants truly cling to the mad fantasy of destroying America. Make no mistake about it. They do. And unless they are stopped now, their attacks will continue and become even more lethal in the future.

To understand the true dangers of Islamic militancy, we can compare it to another ideology which sought world domination—communism. Both movements pursued irrational goals, but the communists at least pursued theirs in a rational way.

Anytime they had to choose between ideology and their own survival, as in Cuba or Berlin, they backed off and chose survival.

Not so for the Islamic militants. They pursue an irrational ideology ir-

> *"Unless [terrorists] are stopped now, their attacks will continue and become even more lethal in the future."*

rationally—with no apparent regard for human life, neither their own lives nor the lives of their enemies. The communists seldom, if ever, produced suicide bombers, while Islamic militancy produces hordes of them, glorifying them and promising them that their dastardly deeds will earn them a glorious afterlife.

This highly pathological aspect of Islamic militancy is what makes it so deadly for mankind.

The Greatest Danger

When in 1996 I wrote a book about fighting terrorism, I warned about the militant Islamic groups operating in the west with the support of foreign powers—serving as a new breed of "domestic-international" terrorists, basing themselves in America to wage jihad against America.

"We must consider the terrorists enemies of mankind, to be given no quarter and no consideration for their purported grievances."

Such groups, I wrote then, nullify in large measure the need to have air power or intercontinental missiles as delivery systems for an Islamic nuclear payload. They will be the delivery system. In the worst of such scenarios, I wrote, the consequences could be not a car bomb but a nuclear bomb in the basement of the World Trade Center.

Well, they did not use a nuclear bomb. They used two 150-ton fully fueled jetliners to wipe out the Twin Towers. But does anyone doubt that given the chance they will throw atom bombs at America and its allies? And perhaps long before that chemical and biological weapons?

This is the greatest danger facing our common future. Some states of the terror network already possess chemical and biological capabilities, and some are feverishly developing nuclear weapons. Can one rule out the possibility that they will be tempted to use such weapons, openly or through terror proxies, or that their weapons might fall into the hands of the terrorist groups they harbor?

We have received a wake-up call from hell. Now the question is simple: Do we rally to defeat this evil, while there is still time, or do we press a collective snooze button and go back to business as usual?

The time for action is now.

Today the terrorists have the will to destroy us, but they do not have the power. There is no doubt that we have the power to crush them. Now we must also show that we have the will to do just that.

Once any part of the terror network acquires nuclear weapons, this equation will fundamentally change, and with it the course of human affairs. This is the historical imperative that now confronts all of us.

Confronting the Terrorism

And now the third point: What do we do about it?

First, as President Bush said, we must make no distinction between the terrorists and the states that support them. It is not enough to root out the terrorists who committed this horrific act of war. We must dismantle the entire terrorist network. If any part of it remains intact, it will rebuild itself, and the specter of terrorism will re-emerge and strike again. Bin Laden, for example, has shuttled over the last decade from Saudi Arabia to Afghanistan to the Sudan and back again. So we must not leave any base intact.

To achieve this goal we must first have moral clarity. We must fight terror wherever and whenever it appears. We must make all states play by the same rules. We must declare terrorism a crime against humanity, and we must consider the terrorists enemies of mankind, to be given no quarter and no consideration for their purported grievances.

If we begin to distinguish between acts of terror, justifying some and repudiating others based on sympathy with this or that cause, we will lose the moral clarity that is so essential for victory.

This clarity is what enabled America and Britain to root out piracy in the 19th century. This is how the Allies rooted out Nazism in the 20th century.

They did not look for the "root cause" of piracy or the "root cause" of Nazism—because they knew that some acts are evil in and of themselves, and do not deserve any consideration or "understanding." They did not ask if Hitler was right about the alleged wrong done to Germany at Versailles. That they left to the historians. The leaders of the Western Alliance said something else: Nothing justifies Nazism. Nothing!

> *"To win this war, we must fight on many fronts. The most obvious one is direct military action against the terrorists themselves."*

We must be equally clear cut today: Nothing justifies terrorism. Nothing!

Terrorism is defined not by the identity of its perpetrators nor by the cause they espouse. Rather, it is defined by the nature of the act.

Terrorism is the deliberate attack on innocent civilians. In this it must be distinguished from legitimate acts of war that target combatants and may unintentionally harm civilians. When the British bombed a Gestapo headquarters in 1944, and one of their bombs unintentionally struck a children's hospital that was a tragedy, but it was not terrorism. When Israel fired a missile that killed two Hamas arch-terrorists, and two Palestinian children who were playing nearby were tragically struck down, that is not terrorism.

But terrorists do not unintentionally harm civilians. They deliberately murder, maim and menace civilians—as many as possible.

No cause, no grievance, no apology can ever justify terrorism. Terrorism against Americans, Israelis, Spaniards, Britons, Russians or anyone else, is all part of the same evil and must be treated as such.

It is time to establish a fixed principle for the international community: any cause that uses terrorism to advance its aims will not be rewarded. On the contrary, it will be punished and placed beyond the pale.

Armed with this moral clarity in defining terrorism, we must possess an equal moral clarity in fighting it.

If we include Iran, Syria and the Palestinian Authority in the coalition to fight terror—even though they currently harbor, sponsor and dispatch terrorists—then the alliance against terror will be defeated from within.

> *"The United States must do everything in its power to prevent regimes like Iran and Iraq from developing nuclear weapons."*

Perhaps we might achieve a short-term objective of destroying one terrorist fiefdom, but it will preclude the possibility of overall victory. Such a coalition will melt down because of its own internal contradictions.

We might win a battle. We will certainly lose the war. These regimes, like all terrorist states, must be given a forthright demand: Stop terrorism, permanently, or you will face the wrath of the free world—through harsh and sustained political, economic and military sanctions.

Obviously, some of these regimes will scramble in fear and issue platitudes about their opposition to terror, just as Arafat, Iran and Syria did, while they keep their terror apparatus intact. We should not be fooled. These regimes are already on the U.S. lists of states supporting terrorism—and if they're not, they should be.

The price of admission for any state into the coalition against terror must be to first completely dismantle the terrorist infrastructures within their realm.

Iran will have to dismantle a worldwide network of terrorism and incitement based in Tehran. Syria will have to shut down Hizballah and the dozen terrorist organizations that operate freely in Damascus and in Lebanon. Arafat will have to crush Hamas and Islamic Jihad, close down their suicide factories and training grounds, rein in his own Fatah and Tanzim terrorists and cease the endless incitement to violence.

Fighting on Many Fronts

To win this war, we must fight on many fronts. The most obvious one is direct military action against the terrorists themselves. Israel's policy of preemptively striking at those who seek to murder its people is, I believe, better understood today and requires no further elaboration.

But there is no substitute for the key action that we must take: Imposing the most punishing diplomatic, economic and military sanction on all terrorist states.

To this must be added these measures:

• Freeze financial assets in the west of terrorist regimes and organizations.
• Revise legislation, subject to periodic renewal, to enable better surveillance against organizations inciting violence.
• Keep convicted terrorists behind bars. Do not negotiate with terrorists.
• Train special forces to fight terror.

And, not least important, impose sanctions on suppliers of nuclear technology to terrorist states.

I've had some experience in pursuing all these courses of action in Israel's battle against terrorism, and I will be glad to elaborate on any one of them if you wish, including the sensitive questions surrounding intelligence.

But I have to be clear: Victory over terrorism is not, at its most fundamental level, a matter of law enforcement or intelligence. However important these functions may be, they can only reduce the dangers, not eliminate them.

The immediate objective is to end all state support for, and complicity with, terror. If vigorously and continuously challenged, most of these regimes can be deterred from sponsoring terrorism.

But there is a real possibility that some will not be deterred—and those may be ones that possess weapons of mass destruction.

Again, we cannot dismiss the possibility that a militant terrorist state will use its proxies to threaten or launch a nuclear attack with apparent impunity. Nor can we completely dismiss the possibility that a militant regime, like its terrorist proxies, will commit collective suicide for the sake of its fanatical ideology.

In this case, we might face not thousands of dead, but hundreds of thousands and possibly millions. This is why the United States must do everything in its power to prevent regimes like Iran and Iraq from developing nuclear weapons, and disarm them of their weapons of mass destruction.

This is the great mission that now stands before the free world. That mission must not be watered down to allow certain states to participate in the coalition that is now being organized. Rather, the coalition must be built around this mission.

It may be that some will shy away from adopting such an uncompromising stance against terrorism. If some free states choose to remain on the sidelines, America must be prepared to march forward without them—for there is no substitute for moral and strategic clarity.

I believe that if the United States stands on principle, all the democracies will eventually join the war on terrorism. The easy route may be tempting, but it will not win the day.

On September 11, I, like everyone else, was glued to a television set watching the savagery that struck America. Yet amid the smoking ruins of the Twin Towers one could make out the Statue of Liberty holding high the torch of freedom. It is freedom's flame that the terrorists sought to extinguish. But it is that same torch, so proudly held by the United States, that can lead the free world to crush the forces of terror and secure our tomorrow.

It is within our power. Let us now make sure that it is within our will.

Reduce U.S. Reliance on Foreign Oil

by Rob Nixon

About the author: *Rob Nixon teaches English and environmental studies at the University of Wisconsin in Madison.*

For 70 years, oil has been responsible for more of America's international entanglements and anxieties than any other industry. Oil continues to be a major source both of America's strategic vulnerability and of its reputation as a bully, in the Islamic world and beyond.

President George W. Bush recently urged America to reduce its reliance on foreign oil. We can take his argument further: by scaling back our dependence on imported oil, we can not only strengthen national security but also enhance America's international image in terms of human rights and environmentalism.

Importing oil costs the United States over $250 billion a year, if one includes federal subsidies and the health and environmental impact of air pollution. America spends $56 billion on the oil itself and another $25 billion on the military defense of oil-exporting Middle Eastern countries. There are additional costs in terms of America's international reputation and moral credibility: Our appetite for foreign fossil fuels has created a long history of unsavory marriages of convenience with petrodespots, generalissimos and fomenters of terrorism.

Coalitions with Repressive Regimes

The United States currently finds itself in a coalition with Russia, Pakistan, Saudi Arabia and the Northern Alliance. Their human rights records range from bad to heinous. This is a conjuncture familiar to oil companies. From the Persian Gulf states to Indonesia, Turkmenistan, Kazakhstan, Colombia, Angola and Nigeria, they have cozied up to dubious, often brutal regimes that allow corporations to operate with few environmental or human rights constraints.

Outside the West, the development of oil resources has repeatedly impeded democracy and social stability. The oil-extraction industry typically concentrates wealth and power and provides many incentives for corruption and iron-fisted rule. In most oil-exporting countries the gap between rich and poor widens over time. From the perspective of local people beneath whose land the oil lies—Bedouins in the Middle East, the Huaorani in Ecuador, Nigeria's Ijaw and Ogoni, the Acehnese of Indonesia—the partnership between oil transnationals and repressive regimes has been ruinous, destroying subsistence cultures while offering little in return. The Nigerian writer Ken Saro-Wiwa, hanged in 1995 for leading protests against such destruction, dubbed the process "genocide by environmental means."

> *"The most decisive war we can wage on behalf of national security and America's global image is the war against our own oil gluttony."*

Oil and related extractive industries have arguably done more to tarnish America's image abroad than any other commercial pursuit. By scaling back our reliance on foreign oil we could reduce a major cause of anti-American feeling while simultaneously decreasing our vulnerability to oil embargoes and price spikes.

Developing Renewable Energy Sources

Long before the September 11 attacks, President Bush adopted the slogan, "National security depends on energy security." How can America best come closer to energy self-sufficiency? To date, the Bush administration has changed our relationship to fossil fuels primarily by deregulating and decentralizing controls, while advocating increased drilling. Interior Secretary Gale Norton supports opening up many wilderness study areas, national monuments and roadless national forests for oil and gas leases.

But we will never be able to drill our way out of even our short-term energy problems, much less our long-term ones. America consumes 25 percent of the world's oil while possessing less than 4 percent of global oil reserves. Even opening the Arctic National Wildlife Refuge to drilling would provide a mere 140 days' worth of fuel. Such modest new supplies would take an estimated seven years to reach the consumer and would be more costly than imported oil.

We have to be more inventive about easing our reliance on all oil, foreign and domestic. A good start would be to reverse the administration's rollbacks in financing research into fuel efficiency and renewable, clean energy sources. We need to build on the encouraging advances in developing wind and wave power, biomass research, transport fuels based on renewable oilseed crops, and photovoltaic modules that can convert even diffuse light into electricity. Some of the most promising progress has been in energy efficiency: household appliances that require half the energy they did a decade ago; cars that can get 70 miles per gallon.

Changing Public Attitudes

Changing public attitudes is going to be an even steeper challenge. Yet is it too much to hope that the S.U.V. will come to be viewed as an unpatriotic relic of the 90's, when America's dependence on foreign oil spiked by over 40 percent? Is it unreasonable to believe that, with commitments from Detroit and government, hybrid cars could become not just more sophisticated but sexier, narrowing the gap between fashion and conscience while saving us money at the pump? Could hybrids and fuel-efficient vehicles emerge as the cars of choice for a more patriotic and worldly America?

Redesigning hybrids is one thing; the business of remodeling American consumer desire is an undertaking altogether more ambitious. But we do have precedents: remember the beloved Oldsmobile 88's and Ford LTD's that lost their appeal after the 1973 Arab oil embargo? With a combination of pocketbook incentives, government stimulus and industry inventiveness, perhaps we could start uncoupling America's passion for the automobile from our dangerous and doomed appetite for oil. The most decisive war we can wage on behalf of national security and America's global image is the war against our own oil gluttony.

Destroy Saddam Hussein's Regime

by Gary Schmitt

About the author: *Gary Schmitt is executive director of the Project for the New American Century.*

Shortly before getting on a plane to fly to New Jersey from Europe in June 2000, Mohamed Atta, the lead hijacker of the first jet airliner to slam into the World Trade Center and, apparently, the lead conspirator in the attacks of September 11, 2001, met with a senior Iraqi intelligence official. This was no chance encounter. Rather than take a flight from Germany, where he had been living, Atta traveled to Prague, almost certainly for the purpose of meeting there with Iraqi intelligence operative Ahmed Samir Ahani.

To understand the significance of this meeting, put yourself in the position of a terrorist. You work within a small cell of operatives; you are continually concerned about security; and you are about to launch a mission designed to bring unprecedented death and destruction to the world's most powerful country. The last thing you would do would be to meet with a foreign official—especially one from a country whose "diplomats" are presumably under close surveillance—unless the meeting were critical to your mission. In light of the otherwise sound "trade-craft" demonstrated by Atta and his confederates in the run-up to September 11, Atta would never have met with an Iraqi intelligence officer unless the Iraqi had been in some way in on the operation.

A Smoking Gun

U.S. intelligence officials have responded to reports of this meeting (and others between Atta and Iraqi intelligence operatives) by denying that they provide a smoking gun tying Iraq to the attacks of September 11. That might be true by the standards of a court of law, but the United States is now engaged not in legal wrangling but in a deadly game of espionage and terrorism. In the world where we now operate, the Prague meeting is about as clear and convincing as evidence gets—especially since our intelligence service apparently has no agents-in-place of its own to tell us what was in fact going on.

This much, however, is beyond dispute: Regardless of the differences between their visions for the Middle East, Saddam Hussein and Osama bin Laden share an overriding objective—to expel the United States from the Middle East. Alliances have been built on less.

And there is evidence of an alliance. For example, there are numerous reports that Saddam's henchmen were reaching out to bin Laden as early as the early 1990s, when he was still operating out of Sudan and Iraq was using Khartoum as a base for its own intelligence operations after the Gulf War. We also know that high-ranking Iraqi intelligence officials have made their way to Afghanistan in recent years to meet with bin Laden and the leadership of al Qaeda. There are Iraqi defectors who claim to have seen radical Muslims at a special terrorist training site in Iraq where trainees learn, among other things, to hijack airplanes. None of this should be a surprise. Iraq can offer bin Laden money and technical expertise, and in exchange al Qaeda can provide the manpower to strike at the United States without exposing Baghdad's hand.

Iraq and Unconventional Weapons

Then there is the matter of the refined anthrax that was used against American Media in Florida and against Congress in the letter sent to Senator Tom Daschle's office. (Both attacks, by the way, came from places visited by Mohamed Atta, New Jersey and Florida.) As Ambassador Richard Butler, former head of the United Nations weapons-inspection effort for Iraq after the Gulf War, has said, "I don't believe that the terrorist groups—al Qaeda and Osama bin Laden—could themselves make anthrax" of this quality. Iraq could. Since the defection of Hussein Kamal, Saddam Hussein's son-in-law, in 1995, we have known that Iraq retains a large biological weapons program. We know it has stockpiled mass quantities of anthrax and has worked hard to make it as potent a weapon of terror as possible.

That Iraq would have a hand in the September 11 attacks or the subsequent anthrax onslaught or both should come as no surprise. [Experts later determined that the anthrax attacks were most likely the work of a domestic terrorist.] Since 1991, Saddam has been at war with the United States, and we with him. The Iraqi dictator has made it known time and again that the "mother of all battles" contin-

> *"Saddam Hussein and Osama bin Laden share an overriding objective—to expel the United States from the Middle East. Alliances have been built on less."*

ues. And, like all tyrants of his maniacal stripe, he seeks not simply to hold onto power but to claim a place in history. As a result, Saddam will never relent until he has had his revenge and driven the United States from the Persian Gulf.

Every so often, we are reminded that the war continues, when Iraq attempts to shoot down an American or British fighter flying over the no-fly zones in northern and southern Iraq and we in turn bomb an Iraqi air-defense site. If this were all the war amounted to, one could argue that containing Saddam within Iraq sufficed for our strategic purposes. But it's not. In 1993, Saddam ordered his intelligence services to assassinate former President George Bush on his trip to Kuwait. Moreover, there are good reasons to believe that Iraq had a hand in the first World Trade Center bombing back in 1993. The mastermind behind the plot was linked to Iraq (via a passport and other details), and a second key figure in the bombing fled soon afterwards to Iraq. Although the Clinton administration ignored the links to Iraq and refused to follow them up, Jim Fox, the FBI's head agent in New York at the time, was convinced of Iraq's involvement. And, finally, we know that Saddam's Iraq continues to pursue development of weapons of mass destruction—nuclear, chemical, and biological—believing that these are the ultimate keys to overcoming America's military dominance in the region.

> *"If all we do is contain Saddam's Iraq, it is a virtual certainty that Baghdad will soon have nuclear weapons."*

In short, Iraq is both equipped with dangerous weapons and out to get the United States. If we have learned one lesson from bin Laden, it is that when someone says he is at war with you, and he has the tools to cause you significant harm, it's no longer enough to say you are watching him carefully. The potential costs of leaving Saddam and his regime in place are simply too high.

Mere Containment Is Not Wise

This conclusion of course is not shared on all sides. Some still insist that we can contain Iraq, just as we contained the Soviet Union for more than four decades. After all, the Soviet Union posed a far greater threat than Iraq today. But this assumes that containment was our preferred strategic policy during the Cold War. It wasn't. Containment was born of necessity—initially, a lack of conventional forces capable of defeating the Red Army in the drawdown following World War II, and subsequently, the threat of the Soviet Union's own nuclear weapons. If we don't have to adopt a policy of containment, we shouldn't.

Moreover, if all we do is contain Saddam's Iraq, it is a virtual certainty that Baghdad will soon have nuclear weapons. (German intelligence believes that day may come within three years.) The question any serious statesman must ask himself is how Saddam, once nuclear-armed, is likely to behave. Will he at that point think we have the stomach to play the game of nuclear deterrence on behalf of our allies in the region, if deterring him could cost us our own massive casualties? It's a risk no one should want to take.

Right now of course the major stumbling block to taking on Iraq in this war, we are told, is the absence of support from our coalition partners for such a course. But that's because they have their doubts, with some justification, that we would be serious about finishing off Saddam. The fact is, the old Persian Gulf coalition began to fall apart around the time the Clinton administration failed to defend the CIA-supported Iraqi opposition from an attack by Saddam's forces in 1996. From that day forward, it was clear that the United States was not really serious, and every state was out for itself. If Washington shows that it intends to get rid of Saddam, the allies who matter will be with us.

There is no question that Iraq has been involved in terrorism in the past; and there is more evidence that it has engaged in terrorism against the United States than many in Washington are willing to admit. But the far more important justification for extending the war on terrorism to toppling Saddam's regime is the terrorist threat he will pose in the near future when his efforts to acquire still deadlier weapons come to fruition. The present war provides President George W. Bush with the opportunity to prevent this from happening. But it is an opportunity that will not last for long. If two or three years from now Saddam is still in power, the war on terrorism will have failed.

Attend to Educational and Economic Needs in the Islamic World

by Tashbih Sayyed

About the author: *Tashbih Sayyed is editor in chief of* In Review, *a quarterly journal published by the United States Institute of Strategic Studies for South Asia, and of* Pakistan Today, *a weekly national newspaper published in California.*

This first war of the new millennium is a war of minds. This war will not be won by conquering bodies and real estate, but rather minds and hearts. This war is to be waged on a different kind of battlefield—in the religious academies and schools. The weapons in this war will have to be different. They will have to change the circumstances that give birth to such a state of mind. We will have to remember that poverty, ignorance and absence of basic human rights give birth to anger and frustration. Extremists can harness these feelings to further their destructive goals.

Those who attacked the World Trade Center and the Pentagon on September 11, 2001, are products of a culture of hatred. This culture evolved over the course of decades and grew out of several sources. To overcome it, Western policymakers should take notice of its origins and vital elements.

The Development of Wahabiism

The most important of these has been the development of Wahabiism in Saudi Arabia, which preaches a very narrow and rigid interpretation of Islam based on its hatred of Zionism and the United States. It preaches that all the miseries that Muslims suffer are caused by a Judeo-Christian conspiracy backed by the United States. In the view of Wahabiism, a global theocratic "Islam" will follow the destruction of the United States and Israel.

Until Saudi Arabia got its windfall of petro dollars in the 1970s, Wahabiism was slow in recruiting its cadre. Its exponents told the Muslims that Jews, with the help of the United States, kept Muslims in economic, social and cultural bondage. They blamed Zionism for destruction of the Ottoman Empire, the establishment of the state of Israel and the total humiliation of Muslims around the world. Wahabiism promises to avenge the centuries-old insults and degradation that Muslims have suffered at the hands of Western industrialized countries as well as Zionism.

Adherents established academies known as *madrasas* to indoctrinate young Muslim minds in this theory. Saudi petro dollars provided the movement with funds to establish *madrasas* in Pakistan, India and Bangladesh. In my experience these *madrasas* have only one objective: to breed Islamic jihadists committed to either convert or eliminate all non-Wahabis everywhere.

Madrasas in Afghanistan

Because of the socioeconomic conditions prevailing in Pakistan and Afghanistan, the *madrasas* have had no problem finding students. By the time the Soviets invaded Afghanistan, *madrasas* had enough numbers to put up an impressive resistance against them. Even U.S. officials were impressed when they encountered in the jihad movement a potent Cold War ally. What U.S. handlers did not know then was that, to these jihadists, there was no difference between Moscow and Washington—both were infidels. They were fighting their war, not that of the United States.

During the Soviet occupation of Afghanistan the United States dumped billions of dollars into the hands of Pakistan's military dictator, Gen. Mohammad Zia ul-Haq, a devout Wahabi himself. He steered some of these funds toward establishing a network of *madrasas* to train and educate future recruits for the mujahideen. He urged the extremist Wahabi Muslims to establish as many *madrasas* as they could and to do this as quickly possible.

Poverty, ignorance, hunger and the absence of basic civil amenities were silent partners in recruitment with the fundamentalist clerics. *Madrasas* instructors conveniently attributed all these ills to the workings of a universal Judeo-Christian conspiracy to keep the Muslims backward. And the United States was cast as the leader of this conspiracy.

The war filled the *madrasas* with new students. In Afghanistan there is only one breadwinner in most families. Thousands of these breadwinners died in the war against the Soviets, leaving behind many thousands

> *"This war will not be won by conquering bodies and real estate, but rather minds and hearts."*

of widows and orphans. There was no social-security system to take care of them. *Madrasas* took advantage of the situation and offered to take these orphans off their mothers' hands. Afghan mothers were only too happy to find that the *madrasas* would take, feed, clothe, shelter and educate their children.

The curriculum was simple: memorization of the Koran, education in the most primitive ways of a very rigid Wahabiism and strenuous military training to fight the infidels. Children in these schools were forbidden to see anyone outside the *madrasas* and were not allowed to watch TV or listen to radio. They were virtually in a bubble totally insulated from the outside world. Day in and day out they were brainwashed into hating the infidels, especially the United States and Zionism.

> *"Uprooting a culture of hatred will mean educating masses of children in Afghanistan, Pakistan and other countries."*

This culture does not owe its existence to any one particular leader but evolved as part of a popular psychology. Virtually all graduates of this culture are ready to die in the process of establishing their "Islamic" state. Needless to say, one may not get rid of the culture by eliminating its leaders. The whole environment has to be changed to eradicate this culture of terrorism.

It took almost 40 years for this culture to grow into a formidable "ism"—Islamism. In this period few realized that Islamism was more dangerous than communism. It has not only conquered Afghanistan but also besieged Pakistan from within. It has exported its revolution to all parts of the world. September 11 proved that even the United States is not beyond its reach.

Socioeconomic Needs

Uprooting a culture of hatred will mean educating masses of children in Afghanistan, Pakistan and other countries. At the same time, education only can be provided in a society that enjoys basic amenities of life—food, clothing, shelter, health care. The provision of these basic amenities in turn needs an economic structure that provides employment to a majority of the people.

Such an effort requires a strategy along the lines of the Marshall Plan provided by the United States to Europe in the aftermath of World War II. To accomplish this goal the United States will have to stay on in Afghanistan after having achieved its immediate goals of defeating the Taliban and capturing Osama bin Laden in order to oversee the establishment of an environment that does not breed hatred. The United States has to help in building socioeconomic resources that provide a bare minimum of civic amenities to the masses so that the reason for their anger is eliminated.

The plan's objective has to be creation of a future generation that believes in the values of democracy, freedom and liberty. Satisfied and content people can afford to send their children to real schools instead of *madrasas*.

To achieve this objective a strict watch must be maintained on what is being taught in the educational institutions in these countries. Islamists took 40 years to overwhelm the world with graduates of their *madrasas*. We will have to be equally patient. While working to counter the extremist mind, we will have to make sure that the affected societies start reaping the benefits of the new Marshall

Plan so that there is a support system available for these new minds to prosper.

Countries receiving aid under this new plan must not be allowed to spend it on defense or pet projects of regime cronies. All programs established under this plan will have the aim of uplifting the standard of living of the masses. Program administrators must show that standards of education and health steadily are on the rise as aid investments flow into the country. Labor-intensive industries should be encouraged so that the maximum number of people can find employment.

True, to ensure that such a plan succeeds, aid-granting nations must keep a strict watch over the benefitting governments. In the past, much of the aid the United States gave for the economic development of countries was misappropriated by rulers such as Joseph Mobuto in Zaire, Ferdinand Marcos in the Philippines, Zia in Pakistan, Saddam Hussein in Iraq, etc., leaving the masses poorer than before. The corruption of these dictators and kings has made the United States a villain in the eyes of the poorest citizens.

However, aid can be dispensed incrementally and with careful verification of distribution, as the World Bank has learned to do in recent years. For a large-scale assistance plan such as this to succeed, its paramount objective must be to ensure that the values of democracy, freedom and liberty become the focus of the new curriculum being taught in the schools.

> *"[The] objective has to be creation of a future generation that believes in the values of democracy, freedom and liberty."*

It is a hopeful sign that Secretary of State Colin Powell, in meetings with Pakistan's military ruler Gen. Pervez Musharraf in mid-October of 2001, reportedly called on Pakistan to do something about the system of fundamentalist religious schools that serve as breeding grounds for militant anti-Americanism and support for the Taliban.

To reform *madrasas*, two steps must be taken. First, the state has to approve the curriculum. Second, a modern and scientific teacher-training program must be introduced to ensure that no person with extremist and fundamentalist views gets a teaching license.

Would extremist and fundamentalist Muslims accept the new and reformed *madrasas*? They would if the state protects moderate clerics ready and willing to issue edicts condemning extremism, which really is the requirement in Islam. Fundamentalists have great respect for religious *fatwas*, and the state will have to encourage them. Islam is a faith of the middle path and rejects extremism in all its forms.

Reform Immigration Laws

by James H. Walsh

About the author: *James H. Walsh served as Associate General Counsel of the U.S. Immigration and Naturalization Service from 1983 to 1994. He has written extensively on immigration issues.*

Three ways to stop foreign terrorists include lobbying for twenty-first century immigration laws, demanding their enforcement, and selecting strict constructionist judges.

To date, whenever the United States has strayed from the Constitution, a historical event has occurred demanding a correction of our course. The September 11 terrorist attacks are surely such an event. Recent years have witnessed a blurring in the separation of powers of the federal government, in no area more than in immigration.

The Congress, whose charge it is to pass legislation beneficial to all people in the nation, instead has produced muddled, unenforceable immigration laws, tailored to appease special interests. In turn, lobbyists of these interests—businesses, farm and grower associations, immigrant rights groups, civil rights groups, and some religious groups—have supported the election campaigns of open-border advocates. The Congressional record speaks for itself; in recent years, each time Congress has drafted a tough immigration bill, special interest lobbyists have rallied their forces to weaken it.

The Executive Branch has fared no better. Over at the U.S. Justice Department, the Immigration and Naturalization Service (INS) and the Border Patrol have abdicated their enforcement responsibilities. By default, they have legalized the illegal entry of foreign nationals into the United States.

Aggravating the situation are federal court decisions that block enforcement of constitutional laws. Such rulings are the specialty of judicial activists intent on setting U.S. immigration policy from the bench. These activist judges place themselves above the founding fathers, as they attempt to usurp the legislative prerogative.

Illegal Entry

How are foreign nationals managing to enter the United States illegally and without valid documents? Those who slip across U.S. borders evade inspection at any port of entry. Others enter on valid documents but then overstay the expiration date on travel, student, or work visas. Some enter on valid documents obtained by illegal means, such as fraud, deceit, or theft. Most Hispanic and Chinese illegal aliens pay large sums to alien smugglers, vicious criminals who escort them across U.S. borders. Arab illegal aliens, for the most part, overstay visas, although some use fraudulent documents at airports of entry, and others cross the land border from Canada. Our neighbor to the north has had a relaxed attitude toward Commonwealth passports, that is, passports from nations that were formerly English crown colonies. These include Afghanistan, Pakistan, India, Bangladesh, Ceylon, and most of sub-Saharan Africa. European and many Asian illegal aliens overstay their visas, with a few crossing U.S. borders on their own.

When asked, the American people are solidly against illegal entry. They want visas tracked and U.S. borders secured. Contrarily, the federal government has heeded special interests that challenge the majority view. As voters and taxpayers, U.S. citizens have the power to put the government back on the course set by our founding fathers—a course that has made the United States of America the oldest democracy in the history of the world. The recent terrorist attacks demonstrated that we foolheartedly risk our democracy by pandering to immigrant special interests.

Getting Congress Back on Track

For the past 30 years, on an annual basis, Congress has produced a jumble of immigration amendments pushed by immigrant lobbyists rather than by the majority of U.S. voters. Immigrant special interest groups have their own agendas, many of which subordinate the security of the nation. One school of thought is that Congress intentionally has made immigration a permanent circus, so as to placate lobbyists and allow them to gain new ground for their clients with each legislative session.

Overlooked is the fact that illegal aliens, by their very presence, regardless of method of entry, are committing a felony. The Illegal Immigration Reform and Immigrant Responsibility Act of 1996 (IIRIRA) was passed to crack down on alien criminals and to expedite deportation. One of its provisions authorized an Institutional Removal Program (IRP) to deport the worst of the convicted criminals in this country illegally. When immigrant lobbyists complained, Congress once again reversed its position. In the aftermath of the World Trade Center attacks, the

> *"The recent terrorist attacks demonstrated that we foolheartedly risk our democracy by pandering to immigrant special interests."*

three-card-Monte that Congress has played with immigration must end. The immigration street swindle is no longer a benign and beguiling pastime of would-be Robin Hoods.

Suggested Remedies

Congress finally must measure the weight of illegal immigration, and the tonnage of the World Trade Center rubble is a damning indictment that demands the following remedies:

Put public health first. Terrorists have the ability to introduce contagious diseases by means of infected persons as well as bioterrorist weapons. Require medical clearances for all visas, for all asylum applicants, and for all those detained as illegal aliens. In the past, legal migration and visa travel required health clearances, and many a person was returned immediately from Ellis Island to the port of embarkation for medical reasons. Foreign nationals, who slip in across our borders, come with no bill of health.

Make enforcement a national effort. Require all federal, territorial, regional, state, and local officials to ask the immigration status of all foreign nationals with whom they deal and to immediately report known or suspected undocumented aliens to a secure federal database. Throughout the nation, government officials at various levels are ignoring U.S. immigration laws to the point of contempt. For instance, a California assemblyman introduced a bill to allow illegal aliens

> *"Congress can make it a criminal offense for government entities to fail to report all undocumented aliens."*

to legally obtain driver licenses, and the sheriff of Los Angeles devised a plan to shield illegal aliens from deportation. Such defiance of U.S. law is unacceptable. Congress can make it a criminal offense for government entities to fail to report all undocumented aliens.

Institute a national identity card. Use corneal prints, fingerprints, or other technology to establish the true identity of all foreign nationals seeking to enter this country. National security depends on personal security. The precedent for national ID cards has been set by unsecured documents such as driver licenses and social security cards. For law-abiding citizens and foreign nationals, national ID cards will entail no loss of freedom or civil rights, and they will help secure U.S. transportation systems and homeland security.

Raise visa standards. In the past, the U.S. State Department, which issues visas, often assigned young consular officers to this task. The war on terrorism requires experienced consular officers in the field to train young officers in handling visa applications by foreign nationals wishing to travel, work, or study in the United States. Centralize visa applications at one consular office in each country and enter all information into a secure database, beginning with the application process and tracking all subsequent information. Check all visa applications against immigration and terrorist watch lists. Track visa applications by code, including a corneal print or fingerprint for each applicant. Set visa application fees to cover the cost of security measures necessary to block the sale of forged documents rampant throughout the world. The task force named by President George Bush to "tighten up the visa policy" can close many potentially dangerous loopholes.

Institute a Foreign Worker Program. Long overdue is a new immigration program to legalize workers, who now enter the country illegally. Congress is discussing the feasibility of a modern version of the World War II Bracero Program that legalized temporary entry of Mexican workers. An updated worker program could issue bona fide foreign workers a visa to enter

> *"Make the [immigration] laws clear and require accountability."*

the United States for a fixed period, such as nine months a year, renewable on a year-to-year basis. Such workers would be guaranteed a minimal wage; they would contribute to Social Security and income taxes, and would be eligible for related benefits.

Reorganize the INS. Long treated as the stepchild of the U.S. Department of Justice, the INS needs some respect, but it won't happen without reorganization and a defined mission. As it stands now, INS has dual and conflicting missions: enforcement (deporting criminals) and benefits (awarding citizenship). Transfer immigration enforcement to a new federal interdepartmental agency, combining the INS and Border Patrol (Justice Department) with the U.S. Customs Service (Treasury Department). The new agency also would include immigrant medical exams by the U.S. Public Health Service (Health and Human Services Department) and plant and animal inspections (U.S. Agriculture Department). Place immigration benefits in the U.S. State Department, which already issues visas. These five agencies currently have a hand in immigration but often work at cross purposes and fail to share intelligence. Reorganization is essential in our War on Terrorism.

Expedite deportations. Begin deportation hearings on all foreign nationals without proper documentation within 72 hours of detention. Curtail the many avenues of appeal and repeated appeal. The U.S. Constitution does not mention special rights for immigrants, and one concise appeal time period and procedure is just. Simplify immigration laws by doing away with such legal-quagmire concepts as "exclusion" and "entry without inspection" that have helped create the current immigration free-for-all. Aliens contemplating illegal entry and the alien smugglers they pay will get the message that no longer can they depend on decade-long delays for asylum claims, legal appeals, and situational claims of constitutional rights. The United States is in a War on Terrorism, and a precedent exists for expedited deportation hearings in wartime.

Ending the Lapse in Enforcement

Before September 11, 2001, there was no concerted effort by federal agencies charged with the enforcement of immigration laws. Years of constant tinkering with U.S. immigration laws have led to a disarray of federal regulations used in implementing the statutes. The result is mixed signals and contradictory directives, top to bottom, with administrators and field personnel hesitating to take any action.

State and local governments, seeing that federal agencies do not cooperate to enforce immigration laws, have chosen to turn their backs on the issue, forbidding their personnel to ask the immigration status of foreign nationals receiving benefits and services. With governmental entities failing to enforce immigration laws, how can private groups and individuals be expected to report immigrant irregularities? End this nation-wide lapse in enforcing immigration laws. The President, who directs the federal agencies, and the Congress, which has oversight and funding power over the agencies, must be tough taskmasters. Make the laws clear and require accountability.

Federal judges have the authority to declare U.S. immigration laws unconstitutional. Short of that, they exceed their authority by blocking the enforcement of existing laws. It is the responsibility of Congress to amend or replace laws. Immigration legislation, if constitutional, is the law of the land and must be enforced, and no judge should stand in the way. The United States and the United Nations recognize five categories for asylum claims: persecution because of race, religion, nationality, membership in a particular social group, or political opinion. Rulings by federal judges who would add gender issues such as homosexuality and female mutilation exceed their authority.

Reclaiming Our Constitutional Rights

Congressional gamesmanship, bureaucratic ineptness, and judicial activism have opened the floodgates to a massive wave of illegal entries. Numbers vary, because currently the nation has no inter-agency database to track foreign nationals, legal or illegal. The recent census projects that eight million undocumented foreign nationals currently reside in our nation. Off-the-cuff estimates by the U.S. Border Patrol put the actual total at three times that number. Until the Census figures were released, the INS placed the number of undocumented foreign nationals at four million. Although the State Department reports that 500,000 foreign students are in U.S. colleges, there is no federal requirement for colleges to keep and report attendance records of these aliens.

> *"It is high time for us to reduce illegal entries by streamlining immigration and visa laws [and] by enforcing these laws."*

It is high time for us to reduce illegal entries by streamlining immigration and visa laws, by enforcing these laws, and by selecting judges who interpret our laws rather than write them.

The ease with which men, women, and children enter our nation illegally has led to a flagrant disrespect for all U.S. laws and for the United States itself as a nation. Undocumented aliens have roamed our streets, safe in the knowledge that it was politically incorrect for anyone, in any capacity, to question, let alone, challenge their immigration status. Today, national security has become a mandate to protect our homeland and to right an egregious wrong—partly the result of our failure to take immigration seriously.

Prepare for Biological Attacks from Terrorists

by Susan Katz Keating

About the author: *Susan Katz Keating is a freelance writer.*

In retrospect, the warnings of the past seem eerily prescient. For years, experts insisted that although the United States was safe from conventional attack, the nation was highly vulnerable to terrorism. In 1996, then-Sen. Sam Nunn, D-Ga., issued this blunt prediction: "It's not a matter of *if*, but *when*" a terrorist attack would occur on U.S. soil.

Now, in the wake of the unprecedented carnage wreaked upon our nation by terrorists on the morning of September 11, 2001, security experts say we must work quickly to shore up defenses against another form of attack that is nothing less than nightmarish.

Biological Terror

"I am convinced that biological terror will strike the United States," said Dr. Kenneth Alibek, who developed bioweapons for the Soviet Union before defecting to the west in 1992. Alibek, an anthrax specialist who now works to combat biological weapons, warned the members of a congressional national security subcommittee that we have much to fear from germ warfare. Said a somber Alibek: "Existing defenses against these weapons are dangerously inadequate."

Those sentiments were shared on the Senate side by Ted Kennedy, D-Mass., who told his colleagues, "Every day we delay in expanding our capabilities exposes innocent Americans to needless danger. We cannot afford to wait."

The American public would likely agree. After a Florida photo editor died after unwittingly breathing in deadly anthrax spores, the country reeled at the news of increasingly dramatic anthrax cases. A tainted letter was mailed to news anchor Tom Brokaw, infecting his assistant. An entire wing of an eight-story Senate office building was closed, and hundreds of government workers were treated for possible infection after anthrax was discovered in a letter mailed to Senate Majority Leader Tom Daschle. A harmless 7-month-old baby contracted anthrax in New York, apparently after visiting his father's office at ABC News. [Experts later determined that the anthrax attacks were not directly related to the September 11 attacks.]

American citizens—rattled by the spate of genuine cases and false bioterror alarms—clearly want some strategy to help repel the attacks. So, too, do experts who warn that the unconventional threat also comes from nuclear and chemical weapons.

Ranking the Threats

How, though, do we defend against an NBC—nuclear/biological/chemical—threat that even now is poorly understood?

"As simple as this may sound, the first step toward defense is to gain some measure of control, no matter how small," says a U.S. intelligence operative speaking on condition of anonymity. "In my line of work, that means you start by ranking the threats. You have to ask, 'What is the likeliest form of strike?' Then you go from there."

Some authorities have warned that there is considerable danger that terrorists have bought old Soviet "backpack" nuclear weapons on the international black market and that such weapons could be used to kill tens of thousands of people at the push of a button.

"Scary stuff," the operative says. "Keep in mind, though, that nuclear weapons come equipped with enabler codes—which are not so easily learned."

Other types of nuclear weapons hold diminished attraction for a terrorist because they are so easy to detect.

"A nuclear weapon gives itself away by its radiological signature," says Washington-based terrorism expert Neil Livingstone. "That signature can be detected." To a terrorist, there is high risk that such a weapon would be found before it could be deployed.

Chemical weapons, while horribly disabling and often deadly, also present problems for terrorists. Chemical agents are awkward to dispense in quantities large enough to cause the numbers of casualties terrorists aim for. Even the infamous sarin nerve gas attack on the Tokyo subway in 1995 killed only 12 victims—an appalling tragedy, but hardly the weapon of mass destruction sought by the perpetrators.

Biological weapons, by contrast, are far more appealing to aggressors. When used properly, Alibek says, such weapons perform as intended: "They work perfectly."

The New "Perfect" Weapon

In the past, Americans had little reason to fear these "perfect" biological devices. In fact, one of the most frightening biological incidents to hit the United States was a naturally occurring smallpox epidemic that swept through Boston in 1901. In that outbreak, public tensions ran high while health officials scrambled to contain an epidemic that ultimately killed 17 percent of its victims.

Deliberate biological incidents in the United States have been almost nonexistent. In the 17 years prior to September 11, 2001, America suffered only two narrowly confined attacks of deliberate food poisoning. A handful of other domestic terrorism incidents from 1992 through 1997 all involved conventional weapons.

Even through most of the 1990s, the threat from biochemical attack seemed unlikely. If nothing else, biochemical agents were viewed as being too hot for terrorists to want to handle.

"Biological agents, especially, are a major threat to anyone trying to work with them," Livingstone says. "Unless you are equipped with state-of-the-art bio-hazard facilities, you are at risk of becoming infected with the agents you manufacture."

For a time, this daunting condition seemed to place the biological and chemical threat to Americans within certain parameters. Only a state government could afford the bio-containment equipment required for the safe manufacture of such hideous weapons. Therefore, only a state could produce them. The only Americans likely to suffer a biochemical attack, it seemed, were members of the military.

> *"We have much to fear from germ warfare."*

That threat came into sharp focus during the Gulf War, after American Special Forces troops captured some Iraqi soldiers. Medical tests revealed that the captives were immune to anthrax. It further emerged that some 6,000 gallons of anthrax were missing from Saddam Hussein's biological warfare arsenal. American intelligence extrapolated from these events a none-too-surprising conclusion: Hussein had loaded the missing anthrax on board missile warheads intended for use against American troops; the Iraqi dictator's own soldiers would not be harmed because they had been immunized.

Thus the United States began a stepped-up military biodefense program aimed at producing vaccines and serums to combat an array of exotic ills. Scientists worked around the clock developing ways to combat anthrax, tularemia, brucella, plague, Q fever and more—including the supposedly eradicated smallpox.

By the late 1990s, the same scientists who labored to protect the military began sounding the alarm for civilians. The scientists worried that civilians—who are neither vaccinated nor issued equipment to protect against biowarfare agents—were glaringly vulnerable to assault. The scientists feared that unprotected civilians might actually become primary targets of biological attack.

Nine of the nation's leading biodefense scientists, including anthrax expert Col. Arthur Friedlander of the U.S. Army Medical Research Institute of Infectious Diseases at Fort Detrick, Md., issued a special report to the nation's physicians. Writing in the August 1997 *Journal of the American Medical Associa-*

tion, the nine scientists described the symptoms and treatment for 10 agents likely to be used in a biological attack.

Anthrax

Among those agents was anthrax, a particularly gruesome disease.

When inhaled, anthrax hides in the lungs for up to five days. The disease appears gently, in the guise of what may seem like a cold or flu. For a few days, the victim seems to get better. This deceptive lull is known as the "anthrax eclipse," during which the disease musters power for a violent, lung-and-brain destroying final onslaught that moves so swiftly that patients have been known to literally die in mid-sentence while talking to their doctors.

The biodefense scientists advised their physician readers, "Once symptoms of inhalational anthrax appear, treatment is almost invariably ineffective . . ."

But even if some light was being shed on the symptoms and treatment of biowarfare agents, much remained obscure.

How, for example, do you know if you've been hit?

"You take blood or environmental samples, and you run tests," says Kyle Olson, a Virginia-based terrorism consultant. "Then you gear your response accordingly."

But that approach only works, Olson adds, if there is reason to suspect a strike. After the September 11 attacks, for instance, the Defense Department and other government agencies dispatched specially trained hazardous materials teams to collect samples from debris at the Pentagon and the World Trade Center. Thankfully, the plane crashes that destroyed so many lives did not also unleash deadly biological agents.

> *"A deadly agent might not be detected until considerable damage has been done, either to afflicted individuals or to the population at large."*

Health authorities also knew to check for anthrax when suspicious powders began turning up in letters sent to news organizations and other targets throughout the country. Fortunately, those cases were identified in time. Potential victims were placed on powerful regimes of anthrax-killing antibiotics.

Preparing for Silent Attacks

But what about the silent attacks that come without warning? Many early symptoms of biological infection mimic those of ordinary colds or flu.

"Unlike the assaults on New York and Washington, a biological attack would not be accompanied by explosions and police sirens," Kennedy said. "In the days that followed, victims of the attack would visit their family doctor or the local emergency room complaining of fevers, aches in the joints or perhaps a sore throat."

A deadly agent might not be detected until considerable damage has been done, either to afflicted individuals or to the population at large.

"This is a problem," Olson says.

Given the right circumstances, the problem could spiral out of hand, with catastrophic results.

When the Black Death spread bubonic plague through Europe in the 15th century, nearly one-quarter of the population died.

The effects went beyond loss of life, says William Bowsky, a University of California history professor who has written extensively about the Black Death. "So many people were killed that it completely changed the balance of power in major institutions and in society at large," Bowsky says.

> *"[There is a] need for increased vigilance over the national pharmaceutical stockpile."*

"It shook up all kinds of things."

Even without killing a fourth of the United States, though, an NBC attack could create social, political and medical havoc. With that in mind, various American cities in recent years have conducted exercises aimed at learning how to handle an NBC incident. The city of Denver staged a mock biological assault. Portsmouth, N.H., practiced for a chemical strike. Washington conducted an exercise that simulated an attack via radiological device. In each case, the cities learned they were not sufficiently prepared.

Dark Winter

Early in 2001, a group of prestigious American think tanks teamed up with a dozen former government officials to stage a mock biowarfare exercise. The exercise, named Dark Winter, aimed to expose problems nationwide and to find ways to resolve them before it was too late.

The exercise, conducted at Andrews Air Force Base in Maryland, began with the President of the United States—portrayed by Sam Nunn—being told that 20 cases of smallpox had been confirmed in Oklahoma. As scripted by Dark Winter's designers, the outbreak was a work of terrorism.

The original 20 victims each infected 20 more. They, in turn, infected a like number and so on, until some 300,000 Americans fell ill within three weeks.

As in the real epidemic that hit Boston in 1901, this mock outbreak sparked enormous controversy. Authorities could not agree on how to proceed.

"In our exercise, the governor of Oklahoma (played by its real governor, Frank Keating) asked for vaccine for every one of his citizens," Nunn said. The "president" refused. He did not want to deplete a national vaccine supply that was already dangerously low.

As the mock outbreak spread, participants portraying state and federal officials argued heatedly. They disagreed on how to determine who should receive the vaccine. Citizens fought and broke laws in order to get vaccines for themselves and their children. The economy spiraled downward. The nation was beset with food shortages. Participants grappled with whether to enforce quarantines.

Most frightening of all was the toll on the health-care system.

In the Dark Winter exercise, doctors and nurses strained to sort the genuinely sick from the "worried well." Health-care workers fell into short supply. Some succumbed to disease themselves or deserted their jobs in fear. Hospitals lacked surge capacity and could not handle the huge influx of victims. The Dark Winter "authorities" had to decide whether to isolate patients in their homes and if so, how to enforce the isolation.

Overall, Dark Winter highlighted a number of new and frightening issues. But it underscored distinct courses of action. Among those is the need for increased vigilance over the national pharmaceutical stockpile, which can provide fully stocked NBC-fighting supplies to any site in the United States within 12 hours. Additionally, the exercise urged that the nation develop plans to handle patient surges at already strained hospitals.

> *"With biological attack now a real and distinct threat, the stakes are higher than ever before."*

In some areas, such plans are already under way. Across the nation, hospitals and clinics are training health-care workers to be vigilant for signs of biological attack. Physicians are particularly on the lookout for the agent [anthrax] that has been disseminated through U.S. mail. At one Manassas, Va., doctor's office, where patients include Pentagon and other federal employees, health-care workers have taken it upon themselves to learn the signs and symptoms of anthrax. Physicians in Boston now have access to a new electronic communications system that allows doctors to report unusual disease patterns to local health officials. Additionally, a number of cities already have made plans to convert National Guard armories and other public buildings into temporary hospitals in case of emergency.

Deterrence of course remains high on the list of government priorities. "If we are attacked with a nuclear, chemical or biological weapon, we need to respond with absolute retaliation," Livingstone advises.

Most of all, security insiders say, the nation must work mightily to increase its ability to detect and disable terrorist plots. With biological attack now a real and distinct threat, the stakes are higher than ever before.

Organizations to Contact

The editors have compiled the following list of organizations concerned with the issues debated in this book. The descriptions are derived from materials provided by the organizations. All have publications or information available for interested readers. The list was compiled on the date of publication of the present volume; the information provided here may change. Be aware that many organizations take several weeks or longer to respond to inquiries, so allow as much time as possible.

American Civil Liberties Union (ACLU)
125 Broad St., 18th Floor, New York, NY 10004-2400
(212) 549-2500
e-mail: aclu@aclu.org • website: www.aclu.org

The American Civil Liberties Union is a national organization that works to defend Americans' civil rights guaranteed by the U.S. Constitution, arguing that measures to protect national security should not compromise fundamental civil liberties. It publishes and distributes policy statements, pamphlets, and press releases with titles such as "In Defense of Freedom in a Time of Crisis" and "National ID Cards: 5 Reasons Why They Should Be Rejected."

American Enterprise Institute (AEI)
1150 17th St. NW, Washington, DC 20036
(202) 862-5800 • (202) 862-7177
website: www.aei.org

The American Enterprise Institute for Public Policy Research is a scholarly research institute that is dedicated to preserving limited government, private enterprise, and a strong foreign policy and national defense. It publishes books including *Study of Revenge: The First World Trade Center Attack and Saddam Hussein's War Against America*. Articles about terrorism and September 11 can be found in its magazine, *American Enterprise*, and on its website.

Anti-Defamation League (ADL)
823 United Nations Plaza, New York, NY 10017
(212) 885-7700 • fax: (212) 867-0779
website: www.adl.org

The Anti-Defamation League is a human relations organization dedicated to combating all forms of prejudice and bigotry. The league has placed a spotlight on terrorism and on the dangers posed for extremism. Its website records reactions to the September 11, 2001, terrorist incidents by both extremist and mainstream organizations, provides background information on Osama bin Laden, and furnishes other materials on terrorism and the Middle East. The ADL also maintains a bimonthly online newsletter, *Frontline*.

The Brookings Institution
1775 Massachusetts Ave. NW, Washington, DC 20036
(202) 797-6000 • fax: (202) 797-6004
e-mail: brookinfo@brook.edu • website: www.brookings.org

The institution, founded in 1927, is a think tank that conducts research and education in foreign policy, economics, government, and the social sciences. In 2001 it began America's Response to Terrorism, a project that provides briefings and analysis to the public and which is featured on the center's website. Other publications include the quarterly *Brookings Review*, periodic *Policy Briefs*, and books including *Terrorism and U.S. Foreign Policy.*

CATO Institute
1000 Massachusetts Ave. NW, Washington, DC 2001-5403
(202) 842-0200 • fax: (202) 842-3490
e-mail: cato@cato.org • website: www.cato.org

The Institute is a nonpartisan public policy research foundation dedicated to limiting the role of government and protecting individual liberties. It publishes the quarterly magazine *Regulation*, the bimonthly *Cato Policy Report*, and numerous policy papers and articles. Works on terrorism include "Does U.S. Intervention Overseas Breed Terrorism?" and "Military Tribunals No Answer."

Center for Strategic and International Studies (CSIS)
1800 K St. NW, Suite 400, Washington, DC 20006
(202) 887-0200 • fax: (202) 775-3199
website: www.csis.org

The center works to provide world leaders with strategic insights and policy options on current and emerging global issues. It publishes books including *To Prevail: An American Strategy for the Campaign Against Terrorism,* the *Washington Quarterly,* a journal on political, economic, and security issues, and other publications including reports that can be downloaded from its website.

Council on American-Islamic Relations (CAIR)
453 New Jersey Ave. SE, Washington, DC 20003
(202) 488-8787 • fax: (202) 488-0833
e-mail: cair@cair-net.org • website: www.cair-net.org

CAIR is a nonprofit membership organization that presents an Islamic perspective on public policy issues and challenges the misrepresentation of Islam and Muslims. It publishes the quarterly newsletter *Faith in Action* and other various publications on Muslims in the United States. Its website includes statements condemning both the September 11 attacks and discrimination against Muslims.

Federal Aviation Administration (FAA)
800 Independence Ave. SW, Washington, DC 20591
(800) 322-7873 • fax: (202) 267-3484
website: www.faa.gov

The Federal Aviation Administration is the component of the U.S. Department of Transportation whose primary responsibility is the safety of civil aviation. The FAA's major functions include regulating civil aviation to promote safety and fulfill the requirements of national defense. Among its publications are *Technology Against Terrorism, Air Piracy, Airport Security and International Terrorism: Winning the War Against Hijackers,* and *Security Tips for Air Travelers.*

Institute for Policy Studies (IPS)
733 15th St. NW, Suite 1020, Washington, DC 20005
(202) 234-9382 • fax: (202) 387-7915
website: www.ips-dc.org

The Institute for Policy Studies is a progressive think tank that works to develop societies built around the values of justice and nonviolence. It publishes reports including *Global Perspectives: A Media Guide to Foreign Policy Experts.* Numerous articles and interviews on September 11 and terrorism are available on its website.

International Policy Institute of Counter-Terrorism (ICT)
PO Box 167, Herzlia 46150, Israel
972-9-9527277 • fax: 972-9-9513073
e-mail: mail@ict.org.il • website: www.ict.org.il

ICT is a research institute dedicated to developing public policy solutions to international terrorism. The ICT website is a comprehensive resource on terrorism and counterterrorism, featuring an extensive database and terrorist attacks and organizations, including al-Qaeda.

Islamic Supreme Council of America (ISCA)
1400 16th Street NW, Room B112, Washington, DC 20036
(202) 939-3400 • fax: (202) 939-3410
e-mail: staff@islamicsupremecouncil.org • website: www.islamicsupremecouncil.org

The ISCA is a nongovernmental religious organization that promotes Islam in America both by providing practical solutions to American Muslisms in integrating Islamic teachings with American culture and by teaching non-Muslims that Islam is a religion of moderation, peace, and tolerance. It strongly condemns Islamic extremists and all forms of terrorism. Its website includes statements, commentaries, and reports on terrorism, including *Usama bin Laden: A Legend Gone Wrong* and *Jihad: A Misunderstood Concept from Islam.*

Middle East Media Research Institute (MEMRI)
PO Box 27837, Washington, DC 20038-7837
(202) 955-9070 • fax: (202) 955-9077
e-mail: memri@erols.com • website: www.memri.org

MEMRI translates and disseminates articles and commentaries from Middle East media sources and provides original research and analysis on the region. Its Jihad and Terrorism Studies Project monitors radical Islamist groups and individuals and their reactions to acts of terrorism around the world.

Middle East Policy Council
1730 M St. NW, Suite 512, Washington, DC 20036-4505
(202) 296-6767 • fax: (202) 296-5791
e-mail: general@mepc.org • website: www.mepc.org

The Middle East Policy Council was founded in 1981 to expand public discussion and understanding of issues affecting U.S. policy in the Middle East. The council is a nonprofit educational organization that operates nationwide. It publishes the quarterly *Middle East Policy Journal* and offers workshops for secondary-level educators on how to teach students about the Arab world and Islam.

U.S. Department of State, Counterterrorism Office
Office of Public Affairs, Rm. 2507
2201 C St. NW, Washington, DC 20520
(202) 647-4000
e-mail: secretary@state.gov • website: www.state.gov/s/ct

The office works to develop and implement American counterterrorism strategy and to improve cooperation with foreign governments. Articles and speeches by government officials are available at its website.

War Resisters League (WRL)
339 Lafayette St., New York, NY 10012
(212) 228-0450 • fax: (212) 228-6193
e-mail: wrl@warresisters.org • website: www.warresisters.org

The WRL, founded in 1923, believes that all war is a crime against humanity and advocates nonviolent methods to create a just and democratic society. It publishes the magazine *The Nonviolent Activist.* Articles from that magazine, as well as other commentary and resources about September 11 and America's war against terrorism, are available on its website.

Washington Institute for Near East Policy
1828 L St. NW, Suite 1050, Washington, DC 20036
(202) 452-0650 • fax: (202) 223-5364
e-mail: info@washingtoninstitute.org • website: www.washingtoninstitute.org

The institute is an independent organization that produces research and analysis on the Middle East and U.S. policy in the region. It publishes numerous position papers and reports on Middle Eastern politics and social developments. It also publishes position papers on Middle Eastern military issues and U.S. policy, including "The Future of Iraq" and "Building for Peace: An American Strategy for the Middle East."

Bibliography

Books

Fouad Ajami	*The Dream Palace of the Arabs.* New York: Vintage Books, 1998.
Yonah Alexander and Michael S. Swetman	*Usama bin Laden's al-Qaida: Profile of a Terrorist Network.* Ardsley, NY: Transnational Publishers, 2001.
Peter L. Bergen	*Holy War, Inc.: Inside the Secret World of Osama bin Laden.* New York: Free Press, 2001.
Yossef Bodansky	*Bin Laden: The Man Who Declared War on America.* Roseville, CA: Prima Publishing, 2001.
Noam Chomsky	*9-11.* New York: Seven Stories Press, 2001.
David Cole and James X. Dempsey	*Terrorism and the Constitution: Sacrificing Civil Liberties in the Name of National Security.* New York: The First Amendment Foundation, 1999.
John K. Cooley	*Unholy Wars: Afghanistan, America, and International Terrorism,* 2nd ed. London: Pluto Press, 2000.
John L. Esposito	*The Oxford History of Islam.* New York: Oxford University Press, 1999.
Philip B. Heymann	*Terrorism and America: A Commonsense Strategy for a Democratic Society.* Cambridge, MA: MIT Press, 1998.
James F. Hoge Jr. and Gideon Rose, eds.	*How Did This Happen? Terrorism and the New War.* New York: Public Affairs, 2001.
Fereydoun Hoveyda	*The Broken Crescent: The "Threat" of Militant Islamic Fundamentalism.* Westport, CT: Praeger, 1998.
Jessica Kornbluth and Jessica Papin, eds.	*Because We Are Americans: What We Discovered on September 11, 2001.* New York: Warner Books, 2001.
Ian O. Lesser et al.	*Countering the New Terrorism.* Arlington, VA: RAND Corporation, 1999.
Bernard Lewis	*What Went Wrong?: Western Impact and Middle Eastern Response.* New York: Oxford University Press, 2001.
Benjamin Netanyahu	*Fighting Terrorism: How Democracies Can Defeat Domestic and International Terrorism.* Collingdale, PA: Diane Publishing, 1998.

William H. Rehnquist	*All the Laws but One: Civil Liberties in Wartime.* New York: Vintage Books, 1998.
Jon Ronson	*Adventures with Extremists.* New York: Simon and Schuster, 2002.
Barbara Shangle, ed.	*Day of Terror, September 11, 2001.* Beaverton, OR: American Product, 2001.
Strobe Talbott and Nayan Chanda, eds.	*The Age of Terror: America and the World After September 11.* New York: Basic Books, 2002.
Robin Wright	*Sacred Rage: The Wrath of Militant Islam.* New York: Simon and Schuster, 2001.

Periodicals

Aijaz Ahmad	"'A Task That Never Ends'—Bush Proposes Perpetual War: The Significance of September 11," *Canadian Dimension,* November/December 2001.
Fouad Ajami	"The Sentry's Solitude," *Foreign Affairs,* November/December 2001.
James Akins	"Why Do They Hate Us?" *In These Times,* December 24, 2001.
Michael Albert	"Operation Infinite Justice? An Interview with Noam Chomsky," *Z Magazine,* November 2001.
Jonathan Alter	"Blame America at Your Peril," *Newsweek,* October 15, 2001.
American Demographics	"What's Next? 9.11.01," October 1, 2001.
Benjamin R. Barber	"Beyond Jihad vs. McWorld," *Nation,* January 21, 2002.
James A. Beverley	"Is Islam a Religion of Peace? The Controversy Reveals a Struggle for the Soul of Islam," *Christianity Today,* January 7, 2002.
Max Boot	"The Case for American Empire," *Weekly Standard,* October 15, 2001.
John F. Burns	"Bin Ladin Stirs Struggle on Meaning of Jihad," *New York Times,* January 27, 2002.
Peter Charles Choharis	"The Case for a Wider War Against Terrorism," *Washington Post National Weekly Edition,* January 14–20, 2002.
Congressional Digest	"War on Terrorism," November 2001.
Harvey Cox	"Religion and the War Against Evil: 'Modernity' Isn't the Arch Fiend, but as Preached by the West, It Appears So to Many," *Nation,* December 24, 2001.
Fred Edwards	"Views Unconsidered, Remedies Untried," *Humanist,* November/December 2001.

Bibliography

Barbara Ehrenreich and Rosa Ehrenreich Brooks	"A Twisted Sense of Duty and Love," *Progressive*, November 2001.
Mark Fineman	"Inside Al Qaeda: A Destructive Devotion," *Los Angeles Times*, September 24, 2001.
John Lewis Gaddis	"Setting Right a Dangerous World," *Chronicle of Higher Education*, January 11, 2002.
Frank J. Gaffney Jr. and Ted Galen Carpenter	"Q: Should the U.S. Seek to Remove the Regimes That Support Terrorism?" (symposium), *Insight on the News*, November 12, 2001.
David Gelernter	"At War—Eight Thoughts on Mass Murder: The Grim Truths," *National Review*, October 1, 2001.
Reuel Marc Gerecht	"Bin Laden, Beware," *Weekly Standard*, September 24, 2001.
Lawrence O. Gostin, Robert C. Cihak, and Michael Arnold Glueck	"Q: Do the States Need Expanded Powers to Prepare for a Bioterrorist Attack?" (symposium), *Insight on the News*, January 7, 2002.
Lee Griffith	"Terror and the Hope Within," *The Other Side*, January/February 2002.
Victor David Hanson	"The Longest War," *American Heritage*, March 2002.
Thomas Harrison	"Only a Democratic Foreign Policy Can Combat Terrorism," *New Politics*, Winter 2002.
Stanley Hoffman	"Why Don't They Like Us? How America Has Become the Object of Much of the Planet's Grievances—and Displaced Discontents," *American Prospect*, November 19, 2001.
Michael Howard	"What's in a Name? How to Fight Terrorism," *Foreign Affairs*, January/February 2002.
Muqtedar Khan	"Understanding the Roots of Muslim Rage," *Canadian Dimension*, November/December 2001.
Carrie Kirby	"Watchdogs Say Terror Bill Goes Too Far," *San Francisco Chronicle*, October 25, 2001.
Charles Krauthammer	"Only in Their Dreams: Why Is the 'Arab Street' Silent? Because a Radical Muslim Fantasy Has Met Reality," *Time*, December 24, 2001.
Michael Lerner	"The Case for Peace," *Time*, October 1, 2001.
Bernard Lewis	"The Roots of Muslim Rage," *Atlantic*, September 1999.
Brink Lindsey	"Poor Choice—Why Globalization Didn't Create 9/11," *New Republic*, November 12, 2001.
Gilbert Meilaender	"After September 11," *Christian Century*, September 26, 2001.
W.J.T. Mitchell	"911: Criticism and Crisis," *Critical Inquiry*, Winter 2002.

Newsweek	"Enter Religion: The Origins of 'Islamic Fundamentalism,'" October 15, 2001.
John O'Sullivan	"Fatal Contact: The Western Influence on Islamic Radicals," *National Review*, November 5, 2001.
Matthew Parris	"Belief in Paradise Is a Recipe for Hell on Earth," *Spectator*, September 23, 2001.
Bruce G. Peabody	"In the Wake of September 11: Civil Liberties and Terrorism," *Social Education*, March 2002.
Richard Perle	"The U.S. Must Strike at Saddam Hussein," *New York Times*, December 28, 2001.
Richard A. Posner	"Security Versus Civil Liberties," *Atlantic*, December 2001.
Sabeel Rahman	"Another New World Order? Multilateralism in the Aftermath of September 11," *Harvard International Review*, Winter 2002.
Adolph L. Reed Jr.	"A Tricky Proposition," *Progressive*, November 2001.
Richard Rhodes et al.	"What Terror Keeps Teaching Us," *New York Times Magazine*, September 23, 2001.
Matthew Rothschild	"The New McCarthyism," *Progressive*, January 2002.
Benjamin Schwartz and Christopher Layne	"A New Grand Strategy," *Atlantic Monthly*, January 2002.
Nelson D. Schwartz	"Learning from Israel," *Fortune*, January 21, 2002.
Stephen Schwartz	"Saudi Friends, Saudi Foes," *Weekly Standard*, October 8, 2001.
Abraham D. Sofaer	"The New Terror," *Hoover Digest*, Fall 2001.
Richard Sokolsky and Joseph McMillan	"Foreign Aid in Our Own Defense," *New York Times*, February 12, 2002.
Jay Tolson	"Early Drafts of History," *U.S. News & World Report*, January 14, 2002.
Sam Howe Verhovek	"Americans Give In to Race Profiling," *New York Times*, September 23, 2001.
Michael Walzer	"Ending Terror," *American Prospect*, October 22, 2001.
Joshua Zeitz	"Are Our Liberties in Peril?" *American Heritage*, November/December 2001.

Index